Acconci Studio

Alsop Architects

Angelil/Graham/Pfenninger/Scholl Architecture

Carme Pinós Studio

Cho Slade Architecture/ TEAM BAHN

Christo and Jeanne-Claude

de Paor Architects

Diller + Scofidio

Eisenman Architects

Field Operations

Foreign Office Architects

Foster and Partners

Gluckman Mayner Architects/ Kohn Pedersen Fox

Gustafson Porter

Hood Design

HTO

Jean-Christophe Choblet

Jorge Mario Jáuregui Architects

Lab Architecture Studio/ Bates Smart

MGP Arquitectura y Urbanismo

Michael Van Valkenburgh Associates

Oscar Niemeyer

Rafael Lozano-Hemmer

RTN Architects

Studio Orta

Snøhetta

StudioMAS Architecture and Urban Design

3LHD

UN Studio

Weiss/Manfredi Architects

Zaha Hadid Architects

OPEN
NEW
DESIGNS
FOR
PUBLIC
SPACE

Published by
Van Alen Institute
30 W 22 Street, 6th Floor
New York, NY 10010
Tel +1 (212) 924-7000
Fax +1 (212) 366-5836
www.vanalen.org

©2004 Van Alen Institute, New York
All rights reserved
Printed in Canada
07 06 05 04 5 4 3 2 1

Editors: Raymond W. Gastil and Zoë Ryan
Design: Flat
Printing and Binding: Solisco Printers Ltd.

Distributed by:
Princeton Architectural Press
37 East 7th Street
New York, NY 10003
Tel +1 (800) 722-6657
www.papress.com

ISBN: 1-56898-470-7

Library of Congress Cataloging-in-Publication Data is available from the publisher

CONTENTS

OPEN: new design for public space
Van Alen Institute, New York

PHOTO: © FLAT INC.

PREFACE

DANIEL L. DOCTOROFF

If past is prologue, there is no doubt that investments in New York's public realm will be the key to our city's continual rebirth. In New York, precedent after precedent indicates that appropriate targeted investments in public space have been the catalysts for the private market reactions that have kept our economy strong. Historically this was the case with Central Park and Park Avenue. More recently we have experienced this with the development of Battery Park City and Hudson River Park.

Daniel L. Doctoroff
Deputy Mayor for Economic
Development and Rebuilding,
New York City

As we move into the 21st century, we can take advantage of similar opportunities, but only if we have the vision to see them and the courage to seize them. In Lower Manhattan, we are in partnership with the Lower Manhattan Development Corporation to invest over $25 million in downtown parks, and we are about to embark on an exciting new effort to re-envision the East River Waterfront. Across the river we are investing in Brooklyn Bridge Park, and are in the process of redefining the waterfront in Greenpoint and Williamsburg. In Manhattan, we have undertaken the challenge of saving and restoring the High Line as a 1.6 mile linear open space, an act that will transform an underutilized neighborhood while reinforcing the city's premier art gallery district. The High Line will connect to a proposed thirty-acre park system that will form the heart of Hudson Yards, a new commercial and residential district that will provide much needed office space, an expanded convention center, a magnificent new sports and exhibition facility, thriving new residential neighborhoods, and much much more. In addition, NYC2012, the committee leading New York's bid to become the host city of the 2012 Olympic Games, recently announced that it is inviting architects to participate in an Innovative Design Study for the 2012 Olympic Village. In every neighborhood in this city, we have left no stone unturned to search out new possibilities for designing high quality public space to attract residents, workers, and visitors from across the globe.

The innovative public spaces featured in OPEN: *new designs for public space* are indicative of the challenges that are being met by cities around the world. Reclaiming post-industrial waterfronts, creating public space in the face of new security concerns, integrating information technology into the public realm—these are but a few of the issues that all great cities confront today, and all do so in a context of limited public funds. In this environment, it will take outstanding leadership to bring public space projects to fruition. Yet we have no choice, for the future of the city hinges—as it always has—on the future of its public realm.

INTRODUCTION

RAYMOND W. GASTIL AND ZOË RYAN

Raymond W. Gastil
Exhibition Director

Zoë Ryan
Exhibition Curator

OPEN: new designs for public space includes projects from six continents that are changing the way we live, work, and play in cities. In the past few years, city dwellers around the world have faced often-terrible challenges to using, much less designing and building public spaces. At the same time, recent history has also underscored how much public space is still valued and vital, from memorials, to protests, to the everyday pleasure of eating lunch in the park. This is as true in Johannesburg as it is in Lower Manhattan: the world is full of sites where memory, commerce, arts, recreation, and transit all command a new investment of time, energy, and resources to build and rebuild a shared public realm. The design of public space, in this city and internationally, will only move forward with an open-minded understanding of how this investment is evolving. The *OPEN* exhibit looks at projects that are recently completed, under construction, or in development, across a spectrum of sponsors, functions, and scales. This volume gives us the opportunity to both document the exhibit's contents and present the broader dialogue that has informed *OPEN* both as it began and in response to the completed exhibit, a conversation that we look forward to continuing as the exhibit travels.

The spaces described have been designed by architects, landscape architects, planners, artists, engineers, and others, together with the individuals and forces that shape and sponsor them, including community groups, government agencies, and the private sector, from street vendors to major corporations. The city in history has always contained intriguing environments created less by design than by accidents of neglect and discovery, and these merit analysis and understanding. In *OPEN*, however, the focus is on projects where that kind of analysis, together with a profound depth of urban knowledge, has been translated into new designs.

It is not an easy time to design public space in global cities. The prevalence of security cameras and security personnel has forced us to reconsider its character. Victor Hugo wrote in the 19th century that the book killed the building. At the beginning of the 21st century the Information Highway has killed the street, the square, and every other public space. Yet there are still buildings, and public space is vital. Camera-filled London has built what is one of the most accessible and visible City Halls in the world. Melbourne has opened a huge arts center whose plaza doubles as the front yard of the city. Tokyo has a new art museum in the sky, at the top of a 52-story tower, offering sweeping 360° views 16 hours a day while in Guadalajara, public space is key to an ambitiously conceived new district. In Soweto, redesigning an historic square as a memorial and marketplace is fundamental to regenerating Johannesburg, while in Singapore, a new "technopole" is grounded by a public space strategy. Macon, Georgia is ready to get an original version of a southern city square, while Genoa, Italy, is determined to make the Piazza San Marco of today. In Rio de Janeiro, public space is the key element in programs of social justice, as in Bogotá, which has an ecological imperative, inserting a greenway throughout the city in an effort to reduce car traffic and create pedestrian thoroughfares. Many of the projects do not fit traditional categorizations of public space. Not all of them are open 24 hours a day, a number charge an entrance fee, some are only partially open to the public, but these are among the real conditions of public space, especially in the 21st century, and rather than ignore the inevitable, this exhibit and publication open up the debate and illustrate the diversity of spaces used by the many publics of contemporary cities.

This is the worst of times to downgrade our expectations for public life. From concerts in Central Park to protests on the Mall, to politics and performance in the streets and squares of six continents, public space is working. Public spaces allow for shared experiences that can give rise to the mutual respect—however grudging—that is the basis of a thriving metropolitan culture. It may or may not be the best of times for public space, but it is a compelling era. Toxic industrial sites are reclaimed, utopian new districts are laid out, manmade islands appear in the river, plazas are put in the sky, and memory, of the good and the unspeakably bad, tries to design its way into the hearts and minds of future citizens. In looking at all this change, it is imperative to try to grasp what is and isn't working, and how "24/7," "innovation," "adaptive reuse," "process," "urban landscape," and "public" are more than catchwords, but integral to unprecedented opportunities.

ACKNOWLEDGEMENTS

OPEN: *new designs for public space* and this catalogue form part of the Institute's core mission, and like our other projects would not have been possible without the input, help and encouragement of many colleagues, friends and other talented and generous individuals. We would first like to thank the exhibit and publication funders, listed separately below, who made this project possible. We are indebted to the participants in the five roundtables held in 2003: Stan Allen, Janet Abrams, Paola Antonelli, Diana Balmori, Craig Barton, Kadambari Baxi, Andrew Darrell, Lisa Frigand, Tony Hiss, Marian Starr Imperatore, Andrea Kahn, Jerold Kayden, Bart Lootsma, Anuradha Mathur, Elizabeth Mossop (who also wrote an essay for this catalogue), Max Page, Anne Pasternak, Sherida Paulsen, Mark Robbins, Ben Rubin, James Russell, James Sanders, Craig Schwitter, Nasrine Seraji, Peter Slatin, David Small, Michael Sorkin, Lisa Strausfeld, and Gwendolyn Wright. Their insightful comments were essential for the exhibition. Thanks also to our sterling essayists, interviewees and commentators: Will Alsop, Ned Cramer, Marc Kristal, Rowan Moore, Enrique Peñalosa, Linda Pollak, Josep Ramoneda, Henning Rasmus, and Deyan Sudjic.

We would like to acknowledge Daniel L. Doctoroff, New York City's Deputy Mayor for Economic Development and Rebuilding for expertly framing this project within the city's bold program for improving the public realm in his preface.

Special thanks to our inspiring exhibition designers: Lauren Crahan, John Hartmann, Troy Ostrander and Cory Yurkovich from Freecell and Tsia Carson, Doug Lloyd, and Petter Ringbom from Flat to whom we are grateful for their unceasing zeal and commitment to creating an innovative design that transformed the gallery into an azure wonderland and a stimulating framework to exhibit these incredible projects—the first Institute show to elicit gasps from visitors over the thorough transformation of our own public realm. Thanks also to the dedicated exhibition installation team: Glen Barfield, Darren Guyer, Mina Talai, Josh Young, and VAI's Arif Durakovic. In addition, thanks to Flat for their exceptional deftness translating a 3-D project into 2-D form with their thoughtful design for this publication.

As always, the Van Alen Institute staff went above and beyond the call of duty in their support and help with this exhibition. For their dedication, we thank Jonathan Cohen-Litant, Marcus Woollen and former VAI employees Alan G. Brake and Claire R. Nelson, as well as the research assistants Michael Osman, Hillary Angelo and Sonya Lee.

Many thanks to the Trustees of the Institute, all of whom contributed to the exhibit with their advice and support, led by current Chair, Sherida Paulsen and her predecessor

Robert Kupiec. Thanks also to: Yona Backer, Susan Begley, Judit Carrera, Pamela Clapp, Oscar Edmundo Diaz, Denise Garcia, Brian Goldberg, Anne Van Ingen, Bob Kapoor, and Sofia Padnos. Special thanks to Princeton Architectural Press and Kevin Lippert for their advice and for distributing this catalogue.

Most importantly, thanks to all the designers, artists, architects, and landscape architects, as well as their inspired clients, whose creative and responsive minds developed the work included in the exhibition and in this volume. Without them we would not have been able to illustrate the wealth of public spaces being designed and built across the globe.

OPEN FUNDERS

EXHIBITION

Major Grants
The Andy Warhol Foundation for the Visual Arts
The National Endowment for the Arts
The New York State Council on the Arts, a State Agency
The Stephen A. and Diana L. Goldberg Foundation

Major In-Kind Support
Duggal

PUBLICATION

Initiating Grant
Consolidated Edison Company of New York, Inc.

and the Generous Support of
Buro Happold Consulting Engineers PC
Elise Jaffe and Jeffrey Brown
Phil and Norma Fine Foundation
Leslie Klein
Susan T. Rodriguez
Ryall Porter Architects

Additional funding for the *OPEN* exhibition and publication was provided by Van Alen Institute

ROUNDTABLE DISCUSSIONS

The following conversations took place in 2003 at the Institute and acted as a frame to the *OPEN* exhibition, helping to guide research and prompt discussion about key themes. These texts are edited and abridged versions of the original transcripts.

CHALLENGING PUBLIC SPACE

Stan Allen is an architect, principal of Field Operations and Dean of the School of Architecture at Princeton University

Andrea Kahn is Adjunct Associate Professor of Architecture and Urban Design at Columbia University

Anne Pasternak is Executive Director of Creative Time, Inc., a non-profit public arts organization

Mark Robbins is an artist and the former Director of Design at the National Endowment for the Arts

MARK ROBBINS: Often what isn't talked about in terms of public space is what most people experience as public space, for example, simulated environments. "I'm in a mall, I'm with people, same as a plaza to me." Most people don't ask, what can't I do in this space that I could in a real city?

STAN ALLEN: Too much control obviously diminishes the public realm, but a certain amount of control is necessary. It's a classic liberal democratic argument. You need a certain amount of control and support to establish the terms of civic discourse. And what are the differences between designed and found spaces? Nobody designed the Brooklyn Bridge Anchorage as a public space.

ANNE PASTERNAK: According to Roebling's designs, the Anchorage was meant to be the national treasury or a wine cellar. Instead, it was used as an open-air playground and market until the arches were enclosed. By 1975, Creative Time began to adapt the space as a venue for exhibitions and events, and now it is closed due to post-9/11 national security concerns.

ROBBINS: It would be interesting to explore public spaces that have been rediscovered and transformed and the guerilla appropriation of spaces, which are made for one thing but get used for another. Though this is ancient history, the cruising areas in the Meat Packing District were a classic. Trucks, which were parked alongside each other at night, made little alleyways, where people coming out of the clubs could hook up. During the day the trucks left and those spaces evaporated, and so did the activity, and at night, it would reconstitute itself.

ANDREA KAHN: Besides the idea of public space as publicly accessible space, there are also political, economic and social notions—the public/private dichotomy can apply to property ownership, to social behavior, it can become extremely politicized. We need to make distinctions between the idea of public space as a place of unplanned encounter, a sociological concept, and the idea of public space as public realm or place of public assembly or deliberation —an idea bound up with political action. It's important to recognize these differences and how often they are elided in our discussions.

ROBBINS: Public space is initially wed to public discourse and dissent, which is why it is so often controlled. No photography, handing out leaflets, playing music, for instance at a mall. There are rules that say "no more than four teenagers can congregate." These recall much earlier laws, which restricted the rights to congregate, because it was seen as a possible prelude to civic unrest. So we do have this image of public space as happy, Cinnabon-scented, good for consumers.

KAHN: Well, one interesting fact is that a lot of design precedents for "good" public space from Western European cities—places like Hyde Park, in London or the Palais Royale, in Paris—were actually designed and used as private spaces, and have had their histories rewritten in order to serve as "great" models for public space.

ALLEN: An example is the steps of Low Library at Columbia University. Especially in the early 1990s at Columbia when we were all talking about indeterminate programs, and here on our front lawn was this space that functioned brilliantly as an indeterminate space. It supports very formal activities such as graduation and then during the spring they set up flea markets in the same space. Political rallies take place there—the unionized workers marched on the steps of the library when they were negotiating with the administration. But it also functions very well as an informal day-to-day space; people sit out in the sun eating their lunch. Now, the interesting thing about the steps of Low Library it that it's a completely classical space, designed by McKim, Mead & White over a hundred years ago. It's symmetrical, dominated by the library at one end. It's clearly not the semiotics of the space that is supporting that complex mix of uses. It's a whole series of more subtle, performative factors—its orientation, where its located on campus (all of the important paths on campus cross through it), its generous dimensions, and even some very immediate, material questions: the quality of the stone that the steps are constructed out of, or the dimension of the treads and risers, which is just right for lounging. But again, it is a totally private space. There are gates that can be shut at any time. So the actual freedom and indeterminacy of that space is in part guaranteed by the fact that it has a kind of institutional support. The power thing can be turned on its head—it is not in the architecture, it is in the way in which people use the architecture, and how open that architecture is to different uses.

PASTERNAK: It's interesting that you talk about the issues of the gates and control, and how people can function quite happily in those public environments. Take my neighborhood park, which is Tompkins Square Park, for example. When the city put up fences around the park people didn't pay any attention to them—they still go and sun themselves on the grass. There are very defined communities within this one park and it's an extremely successful social hub. On the southwest corner is where the homeless people and drug addicts hang and on the northeast side you have the people who perform their tai-chi exercises, play basketball, and work out. When somebody from the outside imposes something on the park it is often resisted by the community. A corporation brought in a sculpture over the summer—it was a wonderful piece of sculpture that I love, but it was done without reaching out to the park community first. So, in part, as a result, park users immediately reacted to its presence and eventually knocked over the sculpture.

KAHN: I was just in Berlin where I visited the new Reichstag Dome. On the ground floor, before entering the building, there is a sign that says the dome is a "public space, everyone is allowed in, no admission charge," but to get there, you have to take off your coat, go through a metal detector, and then get herded into a designated elevator which takes you up to the dome. It is accessible to everyone once you've gone through the barriers and controls, but it is easier to get into a mall. It is easier to get into Potsdammer Platz, which is privatized, than it is to get into the Reichstag. An entirely different kind of publicly owned space are state-owned roadways. Outside of Paris, a new highway was built recently with very careful landscaping and very particular guardrails, made of glass. These rails are highly designed. They make you see the world in a very specific way as you drive past. What you experience is more like a designed highway than a traditional public space, but it is a place that changes your experience. And it was developed as a conscious project on the part of the city.

ALLEN: Your point raises the issue that in general there's a lot more public funding for public space in Europe and the review process is much less cumbersome than it is here. In any city in the States you can't talk to city government and propose public space or a park unless you also suggest a funding scheme that says how that public space is going to be financed and maintained.

ROBBINS: That's why it's important to talk about the relationship between commerce and public space. I would often talk to mayors of American cities about issues such as downtown development, housing, or parks. They would generally lead with something like "we've been talking to some developers, and they said if we did X, we'd get a park, or an active downtown." The problem wasn't that they were using the market model, but that they had little idea of what else in fact was possible. There's a park that was recently built in Columbus, Ohio, and in the distance one can see big bronze tablets obscuring the view of the river and I thought perhaps they would explain something about the history of the place or frame views but instead they were lists of donors.

KAHN: I was in Lisbon in 2003 when they announced the opening of a public square that I realized had been under construction since 1995. This plaza in the center of the city is fascinating formally, because it is actually comprised of two classic public squares divided by a narrow building, which you can move between as if they were one big space, instead of two. They put parking underneath it—a smart, standard European thing to do. As night fell, it became evident that they had devised a most elegant, minimal lighting strategy—embedded into the actual surface of the square. The lights transformed the active square—everybody moves through during the day or hangs out because there are tons of bus stops and tram stops—into a subtle territory that was comfortable to move through but experientially had a completely different quality from the space at mid-day.

ALLEN: One of the best designed public spaces I've been in recently was an institutional building in Chile, designed by the architect Emilio Duarte. It's a kind of Latin American UN, built in the '60s, with all the optimism of that decade. It is a beautiful building, constructed in reinforced concrete, very direct, strongly Corbusien in inspiration, but also making reference to the traditional Chilean courtyard house. Today, although it was designed as a public building, it's almost impossible to visit. The original building was lifted up, in a kind of structural tour-de-force, so you could pass under it in all directions. Now that has been filled in, so part of the essential publicness of the building has been compromised, in part by an architectural change, but in large part due to the climate of security and fear that now surrounds any public institution. Certainly this is one issue, when the very institutions that make a liberal democracy possible become themselves inaccessible, something very significant has been lost.

PASTERNAK: A really interesting and successful example of a public project in the States is Rick Lowe's Project Row Houses in Houston, Texas. In the mid 1990s, the shotgun row houses in Houston were going to be torn down and

Rick convinced the city to give him the two block radius so he could renovate them for single, unwed mothers to live in while offering daycare so they could go back to school, get degrees, go to college, etc. There are herb gardens for healing and vegetable gardens for food to eat. Some of the houses are given over for national and international artists residency studios. This is not a traditional idea of public space, it's personal, residential, and takes the concept of taking a really destitute environment and turning it into something positive for the local community.

Roundtable Discussions

OPEN SYSTEMS

Andrew Darrell, New York Regional Director, Environmental Defense

Craig Schwitter, Partner, Buro Happold Engineers

Peter Slatin, Editor, *The Slatin Report*, Former Founding Editor of *Grid* magazine

Bart Lootsma is an historian, critic and curator in the fields of architecture, design and the visual arts. He is an editor of *ARCHIS*, guest curator of ArchiLab 2004, and Crown Member of the Dutch Culture Council

Anuradha Mathur is a landscape architect and Associate Professor, University of Pennsylvania School of Design, and author and exhibit curator/designer of *Mississippi Floods: Designing a Shifting Landscape* (Yale University Press, 2002)

Elizabeth Mossop is a landscape architect, Associate Professor at Harvard Design School, and author of *City Spaces, Art & Design* (Craftsman House, 2001)

ANDREW DARRELL: We're looking at the intersection of three very large topics: public space, environment, and transportation. A city, for most people, is not something that they think of as part of an ecology or part of the environment. However, cities are both part of the environmental problem, because of their immense impact on the environment, and they're also part of the solution, in the sense that density is much less ecologically damaging than sprawl.

Global climate change is increasingly recognized as one of the larger environmental issues. If you ask, "how does New York affect climate change," the answer is largely through its transportation system. From the point of view of health, 170 million Americans live in areas that are out of compliance with healthy air standards, mostly because of the transportation system–emissions from cars and

trucks. From the point of view of open space, the federal government has recommended 10 acres of open space per 1,000 urban residents. In New York, less than half of the neighborhoods exceed 1.5 acres per 1,000 residents. For many New York children, their experience of "open space" is the hallway, stairwells, and elevators of their apartment complex. The subway system, too, is in many ways a public space, which people use for a whole variety of public forms of interaction. How do we develop ideas that can influence the decisions being made about the future of this city at this nexus between public space, the environment and transportation?

PETER SLATIN: To define "environment" in that nexus I'd say it's a given condition of what's around us, from the macro scale of the city in the region to our tiny neighborhood.

ELIZABETH MOSSOP: That these issues operate at different scales is important, as is the fact that in the North American context, the quality of public space most people live with is incredibly low. There's no overall shortage of open space, but very little of it is useable, and most of it is degraded in terms of environmental conditions and facilities.

BART LOOTSMA: With Andrew's introduction there were issues that are classical modernist ones. It is about architecture and urbanism dealing with collective risks and collective desires. It is about the environment and about the public space. Take the huge politically-supported urban plans like the extension plan of Amsterdam, developed in 1929 and carried out until the year 2000. One-quarter of all the space in the plan is for public space. As planning, it made sense, yet the most difficult thing is how to program it.

ANURADHA MATHUR: Cities in India shake every preconception one has in terms of standardizing any kind of definition of what public is, what landscape is, or what environment is—it begs re-examining every time you step outside of the house. So at one level you're in an environment which one could think of as hopeless, anything goes—or, on the other hand, as completely full of possibility, because there is no regulation. So I would steer away from seeking generalized definitions of public or environmental standards, defining plazas or statistics about open space ratios.

At one level there has to be an activist agenda. On the other hand, we should open the question, concerning the identity of landscapes we take for granted, as my partner, Dilip da Cunha, and I are doing in Bangalore. The city has no major river, and for centuries it has survived on water "tanks," which are reservoirs. There's a slightly undulating topography, and by building an embankment you can impound water.

There are two sort of groups working on these "tanks." One is founded by the Rotary Club, and their postcard has a picture of lakes in Switzerland. The other one is the environmentalists, who are trying to get these reservoirs legally defined as wetlands. The tanks escape both of these definitions: in drought season, people play cricket in them. It becomes what I would call a *maidan*. You extract clay from tank beds for statues for certain ceremonies which go through the dry season. In the wet season they are submerged back into the reservoirs. So it works on a rhythm of being wet and dry. If you define them as wetlands, they would lose their human occupation, and if you make them lakes, they become something to look at.

Another example of the elusiveness of the landscape is in Bombay where one is challenged by seemingly undesigned, vast open territories. Whole families live in one-room houses, and yet right in the middle of these congested districts you have these vast open spaces called *maidans*. They elude being defined as a park, plaza, or wasteland. Today, designers are coming in with aesthetic standards to beautify the *maidans*. Yet it poses the question that Bart brought up of programming. As they are now, they are the ultimate in terms of a self-programming, self-organizing territory.

LOOTSMA: I think one can assume a kind of collective desire to have this access—and when it's so scarce, you have to. In a sense, you would have to introduce regulations that limit the activities that take place there, and enable these different individual spaces to link up to each other, as on the Hudson in New York.

DARRELL: Once you start to link them up to each other, then the spaces that were created initially as parks or public spaces for a particular community, all of a sudden become part of a transportation network for the city, and they begin to connect communities together that had not yet been connected in a very direct way.

MOSSOP: One of the most important things in rediscovering, designing and developing public space is the significance of this integration with infrastructure. It's very rare now that somebody says, "You know, come along, here's $20 million, make us a lovely park." Instead of that, they are more inclined to say, "Well, we've got a massive flooding problem in this district or we need a new sewage treatment plant." So in terms of capital investment, a lot of new public space is being driven by infrastructure. But it's more than that, because the way we're thinking about public spaces is changing, the systems of flows are driving public space.

LOOTSMA: We're talking about collective desires and collective risks and collective needs. We have to be very careful not just to talk about beautiful parks. A stronger case needs to be made for the necessity, but not with a reformist mentality. Cities need to stay productive, to stay healthy, to stay sustainable. In New York City, the opening of the waterfront, and the connectivity of these waterfronts, allows for higher and denser types of living in certain areas. Which actually adds value to the city.

MOSSOP: Some of the most highly-regulated urban environments produce the most mediocre public space. In Singapore they are planned and regulated to death. For public space there needs to be a looseness, because we don't know what people are going to be using these spaces for, even in five or ten years.

MATHUR: The designer's role is to be an activist. It's about finding the right sort of seed to initiate something that will generate its own dynamics and life.

DARRELL: In Harlem, for years merchants had shown up selling African wares along 125th Street, and it became a wonderful bazaar. Yet it became so successful that it became impossible to walk along. So the city took all these vendors and put them in a parking lot. Now the city is calling for an RFP (Request For Proposals) to see how to make 125th Street vital again.

MATHUR: Designers are so good at studying these spontaneous situations, but when they are asked to formalize it, the very dynamism they sought falls apart.

LOOTSMA: There are other types of spontaneous situations. Today, our society is much more individualized than it was when they did the Amsterdam Plan, or when masses of people went to Coney Island. The leisure industry is mainly focused on giving people equipment. People use that equipment, not exactly in the places that we expect them to use it. For example, the most intriguing public space in Rotterdam is the harbor for leisure activities. That's where they go with the four-wheel small vehicles that were designed for the American desert, or they go there for hang gliding. The equipment enables individuals to appropriate places, rather than going to the beautifully designed space where they are expected to go.

CRAIG SCHWITTER: There are problems that require major interventions, and their economics will not be dealt with by the end users, and without really good direction from government, we suffer. We still have a hangover from the Robert Moses era, but we need government pushing ahead. From my experiences in England, the government initiative is there. In the PFI process, which is kind of a design-build process for a hospital or school, the government will contract to a general contractor not only for the building, but for running it for 20 years. This is anathema in the United States, but it gives you 20 years of look-ahead, and could completely change our design mentality.

MOSSOP: For people who are actually in the production end of public space, every single thing, whether it's the handrail, the steps, or using water, is a Pandora's box of liability issues. We brought up new technology, too. Now the new technology that I work with most commonly in designing public space is security technology. It's all about surveillance.

MATHUR: This environment of litigation, driven by defensiveness, tends to homogenize places, too. This issue really boggles me, coming from a country where I'm afraid nobody's accountable, even if something massive happens. (While here if hot coffee falls in somebody's lap, you can win a massive law suit.) There's a certain level of mediocrity in spaces because of all the regulations designers are asked to comply with.

MOSSOP: Another factor that often produces mediocrity is certain sorts of public process. The way that democracy manifests itself in the design process is often part of this homogenizing, fear of change, historicist thing.

SLATIN: Yet regarding Lower Manhattan, where there were some fairly tame designs put forward that, at least as it's portrayed, the public rose up and rejected and demanded design for the first time in perhaps the history of New York. Here you had a public that was rejecting tameness and asking for risk.

SCHWITTER: I feel that public input into these processes is becoming stronger and better because of education or travel or internationalism. I'm not jaded about that process with the World Trade Center. It was a good signal. I hear anecdotes every day from people, my family or friends, or whoever, who travel. They ask, why can't we have that here?

LOOTSMA: But that's the danger. Because you go on vacation and you go to Barcelona, and you see a nice square and you say, now I want the Ramblas in New York. And that's exactly this kind of consumerist thinking.

SCHWITTER: Yet what we are talking about is design, whether in Sydney, Bogotá, Rio de Janeiro, or New York. If you take this idea of New York City as an ecosystem itself, we need to design the city. The pendulum is now in full swing. Design has a process and an outcome, and it's not just about being rich so you can hire an architect. It's about the necessity of productivity.

MEMORY AND THE CITY

Diana Balmori is a landscape architect and urban designer and principal of Balmori Associates

Craig Barton is Associate Professor, Department of Architecture, and Director of the School of Architecture's American Urbanism program, University of Virginia and author of *Sites of Memory: Perspectives on Architecture and Race* (Princeton Architectural Press, 2001)

Marion Starr Imperatore is an architect and directed the Civic Alliance Memorials Committee

Max Page is Assistant Professor of Architecture and History, University of Massachusetts, Amherst and author of *The Creative Destruction of Manhattan, 1900-1940* (University of Chicago Press, 1999)

James Sanders is an architect, screenwriter, and author of *Celluloid Skyline: New York and the Movies* (Knopf, 2001) and *New York: An Illustrated History* with Ric Burns and Lisa Ades (Knopf, 1999)

Gwendolyn Wright is Professor of Architecture at Columbia University's Graduate School of Architecture, Planning and Preservation and author of *Urban Revisions: Current Projects for the Public Realm* with Mike Davis, M. Patricia Fernandez-Kelly and Richard Sennett (MIT Press, 1994)

DIANA BALMORI: I see three transformations of public space that are very critical to the discussion of memory. The first is the rise of the value of the temporary. For me, the Paris Plage project exemplifies this: they took the roadway along the Seine, took the traffic out, put in sand, water jets, palm trees, and platforms for dancing, and suddenly they had two miles of beach. The second is the changing relationship of inside and outside. The Reichstag Dome designed by Foster is an example. You have to pass through security to enter it, but then it is a public walk that takes you up to view the fantastic landscape of Berlin, with a half-way outside feeling. The third is how movement through space is a way of creating public space.

GWENDOLYN WRIGHT: Your primary examples are European; it's hard to have any one of those in the United States that wouldn't be packaged. We should also note how often the actuality of public events that do take place here—and that would include the anti-war protests of early 2003—seems to be denied.

MAX PAGE: I'm glad you brought up the protests because we have this paradox. On the one hand we have the so-called "death of public space." And yet, we have seen millions in the United States and around the world show up to protest the WTO and globalization, and the war in Iraq. On the other hand, just a few days ago we had a vir-

tual march on Washington, with hundreds of thousands of online participants who generated a flood of calls and faxes to legislators.

CRAIG BARTON: There is an element of spontaneity to these places and events that is memorable. One doesn't actually expect the experience that you arrive at, either at the temporary beach—this wonderful juxtaposition of a highway suddenly becoming a place of leisure—or moving through a place where one would expect to have come to rest.

These wonderful new public spaces invent a certain kind of ritual, a new ritual that may be transitory. That's the interesting thing, whether one is trying to create an ongoing ritual that will remain, or whether there's some sense of picking up on local permutations of culture by finding the physical elements that allow them to be much more visible.

WRIGHT: Two rituals that come to mind in New York are the Halloween Parade down in the Village and the Caribbean Parade in Brooklyn, or the New York Marathon, too. They have become so huge that you can't really engage with them anymore. (At least it's a sign of how many people do want such connections.)

JAMES SANDERS: New York has a tradition of taking its commercial facts of life and making them something grander. We can hardly imagine the Macy's Thanksgiving Day Parade now except as a television event, but it began in that earlier spirit. Modern Christmas is a New York invention of the late 19th century—Santa Claus, and the gifts. And the parade takes that to the public space from Central Park West down to Macy's at Herald Square. It's not a question of commercial or non-commercial. It's a question of authenticity.

PAGE: The memory issue is related there. The Labor Day Parade—just one example of these gatherings—began as a political statement of workers. The May Day Parade, which used to be at the north end of Union Square was a huge thing. And they were about the future, but they were also about the past.

BARTON: I'm also interested in those spaces that one bumps into, getting some sense of former habitations, occupations, residences, and traces in New York. The African Burial Ground is one of those places that you bang into and suddenly have some sense of 18th- and 19th-century New York. We have been framing authenticity by the number of people who use the space, but I wonder whether there's another measurement.

PAGE: The Vietnam Veterans Memorial is part of a counter-memorial movement, which challenged the traditional monument, saying that such monuments, with their clear, simplistic jingoistic messages, were the final nails in the coffin of memory.

MARIAN IMPERATORE: A recent model for a counter-memorial is in a residential district in Berlin. There was a tradition of advertising on the stair treads on the stairways to the subway. An artist put plaques on the treads that look like advertising, identifying Jewish merchants and their store locations. As you finish climbing the stairs, you realize that these aren't advertisements, these are people who were killed in the holocaust. I think this is a good example for the question of scale.

PAGE: Maybe there's a kind of appropriateness in a small-scale gesture, which has also been a tradition for memorials: the column, the obelisk, the cenotaph. Because it's the right proportion of memory to useful public space that satisfies two needs: the one to remember, but also to use, and inhabit, and convene.

BARTON: The danger in the Daniel Libeskind-designed scheme for the World Trade Center site is that there's a crystallization of this event. There is no ability for a temporal and in some way a spontaneous transformation to occur.

SHERIDA PAULSEN: Perhaps the Libeskind plan will allow for the space to evolve and grow over time. Effective memorials have to work with utility. The bridge in Croatia [in the OPEN exhibit] is a beautiful example of combining symbolism and utility.

PAGE: One of the things that is lost in all of these designs is the sense, in the early months after 9/11 that we might really rethink the planning and the economy of the city. It has all shrunk to a sixteen-acre site.

JAMES SANDERS: An alternative notion of memorials is that there's not the grand public plaza, but a whole series of places all around the city. Or even forgetting about public spaces, and focusing on public buildings, public investments that might be the memorial.

BALMORI: The Triangle Shirtwaist fire of 1911, in which over 140 women died, is memorialized by fire codes that stipulate that doors must open outward—fire doors all across the world were changed to exit that way, followed by a whole series of legislative reforms.

SANDERS: The US is now building a memorial to World War II on the Mall in Washington DC, but the memorials for years were the GI Bill, and the Veterans Housing Act.

BARTON: The challenge of the memorial to 9/11 has been trying to find a way to give voice to thousands of people who died, who really didn't have a voice in any of the public spaces in New York—or public space in general. The challenge of making contemporary public spaces is to find a way to give voice to an extraordinarily diverse society, which has an enormous amount of ambiguity in it.

WRIGHT: That goes back to the question of authenticity, and how places retain and celebrate history through authentic gestures. My concern—and it relates to Diana's second theme about inside and outside—is that we are too ready as a society to compartmentalize history. It goes into museums or museum-like public places, where we (as designers or historians) put it into neat packages about lessons, meanings, and hierarchies of importance. Hoping to respect and preserve history, we take it away from the messy, unpredictability of city streets and public places. In fact, the city can teach us other things, since it encourages people to look forward as well as backward; it shows evidence of experimentation and alterations, even revolutions, as well as patterns and hierarchies.

BARTON: You have to have a shift in thinking, and see history as a part of an urban infrastructure that is in its own way enduring. It crumbles and it's repaired. My sense is that given the 19th-century paradigm of acculturation, the shift to identity is to find the places that are in their own way resistant. The tension between what's the collective culture and what's the individual diverse culture is what really fuels the interest in making new public spaces.

INFORMATION ENVIRONMENTS

Janet Abrams, Director of the Design Institute at the University of Minnesota

Kadambari Baxi, Principal, Martin/Baxi Architects, and ImageMachine

Lisa Strausfeld, Partner, Pentagram, and Principal, InformationArt

David Small, Principal and Founder, Small Design Firm

Michael Sorkin, Michael Sorkin Studio, and Professor of Architecture and Director of the graduate urban design program at New York's City College

JANET ABRAMS: If we take *Learning from Las Vegas* (Robert Venturi, Steven Izenour, Denise Scott Brown, MIT Press, 1977) as a benchmark, what is substantially different today about media in public space? Is it a matter of technology, or siting, or the proliferation of data from other sources besides the large-scale? Can we consider not just projected data, but also the realm of private gadgets/public spaces/public encounters? And who's sending messages to whom?

MICHAEL SORKIN: Speaking in terms of New York, nobody can have missed the Times Square-ification of virtually everywhere in the city. Particularly invidious of these semi-transparent membranes that are hung over facades is their impact on the public realm. There is a decline in the sense of civil respect for vertical surfaces.

ABRAMS: Who's supposed to be paying that respect?

SORKIN: I would like to talk about a notion of decorum in the city, which is conventional, not codified legally, but certainly codified in the habits of citizens. There is also an expansion and contraction of the question of the private in the city. The decorum that forms a kind of envelope around private space is yielding to other demands. There is a selfishness in the willingness to intervene in realms otherwise thought public by private interests—any surface of the city is up for grabs in terms of advertising. This extends to both the advertising signals that occlude buildings, and the willingness of people to intrude on the private territory of other citizens in places like the elevator or on the street by talking on their cell phones.

ABRAMS: Gert Staal, the editor of *ITEMS*, the Dutch design magazine, describes this disruption of the bubble of personal space as a kind of leakage. Some people consider it offensive, but so many of us take part in that behavior that it seems almost anachronistic to complain about it. What has been lost and what might have been gained? What's the difference between hearing about other people's lives by overhearing their cell phone conversations or just overhearing a face-to-face conversation in an elevator?

SORKIN: This bubble of personal space is a fairly hoary way of describing the nature of public and private domains and their interactions. This is very much culturally based.

KADAMBARI BAXI: I agree. It would be interesting to explore how much of it is a cultural difference. People use cell phones very differently in other cities and countries. Here, you hear people talking about their private life in a restaurant. You would never hear that in India but you would hear a very big, elaborate conversation about food. These are interesting cultural dimensions that are never going to change.

ABRAMS: Going back to billboards and other signage on the streets, does everything that is projected have to be entertaining?

LISA STRAUSFELD: I think it has to do with how these things are sited; literally where they go and what their role is. For me, information in public space is more about connection and community. At best there are examples such as the 1962 CBS broadcast of John Glenn going into orbit in Grand Central Station. This transit space, with an infinite circulation of traffic, suddenly became a theater and gave way to a shared experience. These types of experiences are incredibly powerful.

BAXI: Are there other models of public-private partnerships for those vertical surfaces besides the purely commercial? They could be similar to the zoning incentives, which were given to developers: they could build higher if they kept public space at the bottom. The same kind of incentive could be applied to projecting information in a non-commercial way, which could be incredibly valuable to the public realm.

SORKIN: There are power imbalances in this culture. I've always been kind of interested in the idea that there is an equal time regulation for political speech on the airwaves, but no equal time regulation for commercial speech.

STRAUSFELD: For one public transportation client, we of course had to take care of advertising and retail information but we proposed a lot of civic content. We were interested in conveying a transparent democracy by showing what was going on in congress; what bills were going through, voting records.

SORKIN: It is not simply a question of access to various forms of speech, but privacy and protection as well. In New York, it's almost impossible to walk down the street without being assaulted by a message in which I have no interest.

ABRAMS: That doesn't seem so very different from how it has been for centuries. When you look at pictures of New York in 1890 it was stuffed with information: there were tons of graphics, in terms of signage layered vertically and horizontally, all over the facades of buildings. What has changed, exponentially, is the cost of the technology, and the impulse to somehow fund it through commercial revenue.

DAVID SMALL: If we think about private messages, there are interesting times where the public takes over public space such as right after September 11 when suddenly every surface was covered with these personal, public messages of missing people. The public suddenly took ownership of public spaces in the city. Maybe the best that technology could do, would be to support that kind of public action, which doesn't require authority to allow it to happen. No political process had to be gone through, that space was just suddenly available to everybody.

STRAUSFELD: I was also thinking of the banners that people produced for the recent peace rallies. There's plenty of information technology out there, but they used cardboard and the pavement.

SMALL: But that required a lot of hardware and construction too. The messages after 9/11 depended on the fact that people had their family photos on computers and a color printer. Ten years ago people would have had a much harder time actually getting those posters out.

STRAUSFELD: I think that there's been a continuum. Information on public buildings has always been at the façade level where there's a public face of shared experience and the building participates in public space. One thing that's changed is that the volume has been turned up, in terms of the brightness and the fact that the information now changes over time. The other thing that's different is our expectations—we now want to be immersed in information all the time, and feel that information should be available and accessible, and be right there in the environment.

ABRAMS: Has the experience of community as in physical space been supplanted over the course of the 20th century by the shared experience of knowledge in a media environment? There seems to be a sense of loss that space no longer has the power to incarnate us in public as a community, and has perhaps given way to other expressions of belonging.

SORKIN: I firmly believe that one of the constituent elements of a kind of democratic, urban polity is accident: a set of accidental encounters in which you meet somebody in the street, you encounter something new, you get lost, whatever it is. This is part of the dynamics of choice—it's constantly opened in some way. My impression of many of the technological encounters today, the regime of surveillance, for example, is that they are occluding accident.

ABRAMS: However, one could argue, conversely, that the accident of meeting someone you might find congenial could actually be augmented by technology. For example, the British designers Dunne and Raby were recently commissioned by the European Union to explore the relationship between the urban environment and cell phone use. They filtered information that participants had previously entered on an online database and transferred certain bits to their cell phones—so that when you are in a public space and surrounded by other people your cell phone can prompt you if somebody in your vicinity has similar preferences.

SORKIN: I think these kinds of pedestrian compatible media that slightly enhance urban life add to the mix in the street as opposed to the historic culture of separation of modes.

SMALL: Part of the renovation project that we are working on for the Mary Baker Eddy Library for the Betterment of Humanity involves using projections for non-advertising purposes as part of an exhibition to celebrate the power of ideas to inspire and transform. The projections are completely typographic and take the form of quotes on a range of topics from democracy, freedom, love or sin and are meant to inspire people with ideas and beliefs from different cultures.

ABRAMS: I'm curious about the economy of attention that's at play here. I wonder what's already known, what's being measured, and what is merely being guessed about how people actually perceive and spend time with this kind of dynamic inscription?

SMALL: We deliberately paced the information so that

is does not seem like an advertising message. By slowing it down you have to wait a while for the next quote. We were able to encourage a certain pacing and a certain mode of reflection, which is usually the opposite of what you're trying to do with projected messages where you're trying to attract people's attention with a lot of information that changes quickly.

BAXI: What is interesting about technology is its potential to give control to the users so they can block off what they don't want to see and just have access to what they want.

STRAUSFELD: I've been thinking a lot about the pro-gramming of content. There's the scale of space but then there's the scale of information and content. The John Glenn orbit, for example, or the events of September 11 are events that are at the scale of public space. And then there are things that happen, events of a smaller scale where you can almost imagine them being mapped to smaller groups of interest. It is the combination of the shared moment, content, life event, and the space and the way these work together that makes public spaces exciting.

LEISURE AND POLITICS

Sherida Paulsen is a partner at Pasanella + Klein Stolzman + Berg Architects, and former Chair of the New York City Landmarks Preservation Commission

Lisa Frigand is a program manager of economic development at Con Edison

Paola Antonelli is Curator, Architecture & Design at the Museum of Modern Art, New York

Tony Hiss is an independent author, lecturer, and consultant on restoring America's cities and landscapes, and a Visiting Scholar at the Robert F. Wagner Graduate School of Public Service, New York University

Jerold Kayden is a lawyer and city planner, and Associate Professor of Urban Planning at the Harvard Design School

Ben Rubin is a sound designer and multimedia artist. He is the director of EAR Studio, a multimedia design and technology firm in New York City that he founded in 1993

Nasrine Seraji is an architect, and Professor and Chair of the Department of Architecture at Cornell University in Ithaca, New York

TONY HISS: There's a front-page story in *The New York Times* today, New York City and New York State are getting $8 billion of federal money to make security changes to the city as a result of September 11, and they're talking about hardening Grand Central Station and Penn Station, Port Authority Bus Terminal, and the George Washington Bridge. These are all major public spaces of the city. There was fear of crime in the 1980s. The response was put gates on shop windows and put razor wire on top of walls. And this certainly had an incredible effect on the feeling of the city, whether or not it had an effect on the crime rate. So I hope we don't do that again. But we really haven't begun to grapple with the meaning of what security in public spaces is.

PAOLA ANTONELLI: Coming from Europe, one of the first things that you notice about the United States is the enormous need to regulate social life and private life as a consequence. Most recently it is the smoking ban in bars and restaurants in New York City. Why do people need to regulate so much? In a way it's a form of mistrust of your fellow human beings if you think of it in an idealistic way. On the other hand it's a very pragmatic choice. You avoid lawsuits. Public spaces become zones of higher regulation as opposed to zones of recreation.

LISA FRIGAND: When you ask about the impact of security, there's hard security, and there's perceived security. I remember there were several panels convened not long after September 11 and the issue came up that people had naturally gravitated to parks on that day. Open spaces on some level would be considered very vulnerable, and yet people felt safe because they were communicating with each other and they were together.

NASRINE SERAJI: I think that as long as publicness is perceived as a privilege and not a right, one is going to be faced always with regulatory measures. They have to be there in order to define what is and isn't public. In the United States, we still perceive architecture, urbanism, and design as a privilege, and one has the right to it only in certain social categories.

HISS: I found an interesting article the other day from 1954 published in the *Bulletin of the Atomic Scientists*. It was a planning article called "The Dispersal of Cities as a Defense Measure." And it was one of the early articles arguing for an interstate highway system for defense purposes, saying that …

ANTONELLI: … sprawl is good.

HISS: Yes, sprawl was, in fact, according to this way of thinking, going to save us because too many of our decision makers were concentrated in 12 urban areas, and long-range missiles could knock us out. A lot of what we've done has been because of fear and not because of trying to see how you adapt a strong public place to change a situation. And now the new perception, of course, is that anything can become a bomb at any moment.

JEROLD KAYDEN: The security issue presents three possible states of engagement for the non-security oriented professional. One is what I would call the "oppositional" state of engagement. The second is what I might term the "post-participatory" state of engagement, which is to prettify road barriers with paint and foliage. The third state of engagement is the one that's most interesting, which is to "engage at the creation."

BEN RUBIN: As far as I'm aware, there's very little in the way of a public review of security measures. Personally, I find myself enormously depressed whenever I have to pass through a checkpoint or see barriers around. There's a kind of implied narrative to each of these security devices, whether it's a road-side barrier or a metal detector, that anyone who's observant and sees these things and has an imagination will start to imagine a truck trying to drive through with a bomb or you see a metal detector and imagine people trying to enter the building. I think there's a psychic cost.

HISS: Ben's concerns are valid. We need to find a way of measuring psychic loss instead of just saying, well, it hasn't been done before. There is a discipline that's been around for years, which started with Oscar Newman's defensible space idea that has evolved into Crime Prevention Through Environmental Design, or CPTED. The idea is that instead of punitive control, meaning policemen, you can get people to regulate their own behavior in public spaces through self-control. The idea goes back to Jane Jacobs, and so-called natural surveillance, that if there are many eyes on a place it tends to feel more secure, and people behave in a more secure way if you maximize how much people can see within a public space.

SHERIDA PAULSEN: These principles go back further to Frederick Law Olmsted's concept of Central Park. The design was conceived to reinforce certain behaviors to promote cleanliness and sanitation. These ideas were being integrated in the design of public space even then.

SERAJI: We are becoming more cynical in architecture, and cynicism only allows for the post-participatory response to security issues as opposed to the visionary, upfront approach.

KAYDEN: We still have the task of defining what public space is. We're hearing two strong articulations of what public space is: one is regulated and one is anarchic and sort of chaotic. [The discussion ranged from Central Park to Times Square.]

HISS: I have my own metrics or purposes for public space. The first is perhaps utilitarian, the provision of passive and active recreational public spaces like Central Park. A second purpose is community, to encourage tolerance, inclusiveness, and acceptance. A third is democracy, and those two frequently get thrown together, but democracy, I think, has more to do with people meeting together as equals in order to find solutions to common problems. And the fourth I frequently talk about is the symbolic, the iconic, the aesthetic, the visual—that "extra dimension" that evokes and provokes new thoughts and feelings and capacities in us. Yet now we not only need to think about security differently, we also need to think about the planet differently.

ANTONELLI: So it's time to be visionary. Can you have vision and democracy at the same time in public spaces?

SERAJI: Of course you can. It is important to look at what isn't inherent and is invisible in architecture. For example, if we take technology. I would love to see a design of a public square that takes noise into consideration in such a way that you don't hear cell phones ringing and somebody else talking. Perhaps it is in the design of surfaces or forms or the way public space is organized. As soon as we begin to reexamine the contemporary form of a series of 19th-century and early 20th-century visions it is possible to be creative.

KAYDEN: What are the qualities of experience that we can say would be desirable in a public space?

RUBIN: There's some beautiful documentation that was produced by Robert Irwin when he was hired to produce a public art master plan for the Miami Airport. He worked on it for years and produced some beautiful principles for not only public art, but public space and design in general. I remember a few of them: delight, surprise, and slowing down people and their experience of time. He created a framework for thinking about public space that was entirely based on experience. He created a two-pronged chart with design concerns on one prong, and experience and art concerns on the other, and looked at interrelating them both on a practical level of what does an airport need to do and what are the opportunities that it can provide? It can entertain them as they wait, it can delight them as they move through the space.

ANTONELLI: We're all going back to the principle of a design, which has a strong idea and balancing the means and the goals.

PAULSEN: But I think it's about articulating a set of goals, which I don't think from a regulatory point of view we have done. We specify how to measure public space by how many linear feet of benches there are or how many square feet of plaza area, etc. But there's nothing in there about the experience.

ANTONELLI: How can you regulate that?

PAULSEN: Well that's the challenge. Is it an experience or is it goal-oriented? How could we come up with some descriptive words? There are a number of issues that are being looked at for Lower Manhattan regarding quality of life. What kind of environment are we trying to provide in Lower Manhattan? And the goals may not be mutually supportive unless somebody actually articulates them.

HISS: I would like to see 21st-century public spaces begin to work on the question of how can such spaces help us sense and connect to others beyond our local or "home" communities, and connect, too, to the biosphere. I also urge us to start thinking about a connected system of public spaces rather than just thinking about "public space" as a single entity. Holding all the many kinds of public spaces together in the mind is hugely important.

SERAJI: One of the problems I find is that everyone thinks that public spaces these days have a very specific function. It's almost as if as human beings we are losing the capacity to sit somewhere and reflect, or just concentrate.

HISS: Can a public space be created in such a way that activities will spontaneously emerge within them, like a square in which people start playing chess?

SERAJI: Yes, look at the Parc Citroen in Paris in a formerly polluted area. There are herb gardens in the city where nobody would think of putting them—it is a provocative idea. People want to lie there. So there are activities that programmatically can allow for the generation of other programs.

HISS: That's a mark of good design—it allows for the emergence of new activities that the designers themselves haven't even thought of.

THE PLAZA UNBOUND

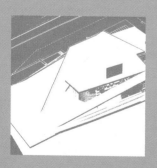   

For generations of northern Americans, the traditional public spaces of Europe and Latin America, whether called plazas, places, or piazzas, were beacons of a better urban life. The Americans longed to live in a city where there was a place to go, on foot instead of by car, that was neither the commercial street nor the green recreational park. In the second half of the 20th century, many cities tried to create such spaces: New York did this by choice and policy with the "plaza bonus," which allowed developers to erect higher buildings in return for public space at or close to ground level. Despite some celebrated exceptions, the results didn't generally match the expectations of a new urbanity fueled by trips to Venice and Oaxaca. Nonetheless, there has been a cultural shift, engendering a renewed era of active parks, sidewalks, and even some plazas. The very recent flood of security fears combined with seemingly unlimited varieties of "place-less" telecommunications threatened to erode this shift, and even erase the plaza from the future of the city. Instead, the plaza is being reinvented, from Europe to the South Pacific.

In **Genoa, Italy** the soon-to-break-ground Ponte Parodi promises a three-dimensional, 24/7 (or at least 18/7) site that thrusts the plaza into the middle of the harbor, combining the functions of what might once have been a recreation pier with a full range of commerce, media, and sport. It is organized into overlapping layers whose form simulates not a traditional urban square, but rather creates an asymmetrical space carved out of a landscape. Meanwhile, in **London, United Kingdom,** the now-open Greater London Authority Headquarters (City Hall), instead of shielding local government behind security barriers, sets it on a prominent waterfront site. There are outdoor public spaces at the base, connecting to a pedestrian walkway, but most importantly the plaza is pulled inside into spiraling ramps rising to the city's "Living Room." In **Melbourne, Australia,** Federation Square now performs several tasks—it covers the railroad cut and services rail passengers, connects the city to the river, contains major cultural programs, and through all this yields the indoor/outdoor plaza that Melbourne never knew it needed for activities from peace protests to watching football matches. In **Oslo, Norway,** the new Opera House will be an "indoor" building whose "outdoor" skin turns into a sloping landscape, cutting right through land and water as it slides into the harbor. The level of access and transparency varies, but all of these plazas are designed with an open-minded attitude towards the public's relationship to arts, government, and recreation, a 20th-century goal still worth building for.

OSLO NATIONAL OPERA HOUSE

OVERVIEW

Oslo-based architecture firm Snøhetta won the open, international competition to design the National Opera House for Den Norske Opera in 2000. Their design reinterprets traditional opera house buildings that conventionally limit their public spaces to exterior plazas or grand lobbies, often only accessible during open hours, by making the rooftop that slopes to meet an adjacent waterfront plaza accessible to the public as a viewing platform and recreation area. The location of the building, currently under construction and due to be completed in 2007, east of the city center on a former industrial dockside has been chosen specifically as a way to invigorate development in this area, taking advantage of the spectacular views of the water and the city.

Sixty to seventy percent of Norway's population attends operatic performances every year but the country has never had a national opera house. The request for design proposals put out by the opera company in 1999 generated 240 entries from around the world, which were exhibited in an airplane hangar in the former Fornebu airport on the outskirts of the city. The public was invited to vote on the designs, the results of which were integrated into the final decision. Snøhetta's design was seen to most fittingly address the competition brief, which had stipulated that the building should have a prominent design that could accommodate the functions of a performance space and stimulate development along the waterfront.

DESIGNERS

Snøhetta is a 22-person office with architects, landscape architects and interior designers on staff, led by Craig Dykers, Christoph Kapeller and Kjetil Traedal Thorse. Famed for their design for the new 800,000-square-foot library in Alexandria, Egypt, that opened its doors in 2002, Snøhetta is practiced in creating buildings that have an explicit relationship with their surroundings. The sloped form of the library mirrors the surrounding landscape and a large reflecting pool and public plaza connect the building to the nearby Mediterranean Sea and the city of Alexandria. With the Oslo National Opera House Snøhetta reintroduces the coastline into the city.

DESCRIPTION

Although over half the population attends performances, Snøhetta was keen to incorporate a legitimate public space that would attract people who might not otherwise visit the opera house and further stimulate the economy in the eastern edge of the city. The white roof terrace that radically descends into the fjord singled out Snøhetta's design from the other competition entries. The 126,000-square-foot roof terrace ramps over the entire building from the main plaza in front of the opera. Rising over the entrance foyer that faces the city center and the two opera halls that seat 1,350 and 400, the roof platform forks around the 115-foot-high central tower of the main auditorium and glass covered lobby, which can be viewed from above. Cantilevering over the back of the building, which has 300,000-square-feet of support space for the opera, the terrace forms a plaza at ground level before sliding down into the water.

OUTLOOK

Snøhetta's monumental design is a striking artificial landscape that provides a unique waterfront terrace with panoramic views that can be enjoyed by a diverse public, whether opera-goers or not. Mimicking the natural line of the coast, it visually and physically connects to Oslo's characteristic topography blurring the line between natural and manmade. The sweeping form of the building not only creates a unique identity for the opera house and a contemporary icon for Oslo but introduces a new type of architectural landscape that gives locals and tourists alike a new public space that can be used 24 hours a day.

View of National Opera House, looking northeast

RENDERING: SNØHETTA

Aerial view of Oslo National Opera House showing rooftop plaza

RENDERING: SNØHETTA

"Monuments have conventionally been seen as dominating artifacts that 'look down' on the people visiting them. They are not seen as allowing for experience; rather they have been thought to dictate experience. We wanted to create a contemporary monument; a social monument allowing differing types of people to experience the building in their own manner, while still creating a lasting memory in the city of the imagination."

CRAIG DYKERS, SNØHETTA

FEDERATION SQUARE

MELBOURNE, AUSTRALIA
LAB ARCHITECTURE STUDIO WITH BATES SMART

OVERVIEW

Federation Square in central Melbourne, a 9-acre former industrial zone with two enormous commercial buildings later demolished, was identified by the Australian government in the late 1980s as the site for a new museum and arts complex. On the banks of the River Yarra, the site is decked over operational railway lines between the towers of the central business district to the north and the river to the south, the Melbourne Cricket Ground to the east and the Flinders Street Station to the west. The competition brief released in 1995 required that the square, the size of a city block, incorporate almost 145,000 square feet of commercial and cultural space. These include the Australian Center for the Moving Image with its own offices, cinema, studios and screen-based galleries; offices and recording studios for SBS, a public broadcasting service; as well as restaurants, cafés and auxiliary offices. In addition to the heterogeneous program of buildings, the brief stipulated that a civic square with the capacity to accommodate 25,000 people in an open-air amphitheater should be the focal point of the project.

DESIGNERS

Lab Architecture Studio (then based in London), led by Peter Davidson and Donald Bates, won the two-stage, open international design competition for Federation Square in 1997 and immediately relocated to Melbourne. This, their first major commission, was a collaboration with the Melbourne-based firm Bates Smart.

DESCRIPTION

Planned to open in 2000 to mark the centenary of Australia's federation, the square opened in 2002. Design and engineering challenges, changes in government administration, and budget constraints were some of the factors that caused the delay, as well as government additions to the brief after the selection of the winning entry. These included adding the National Gallery of Victoria to the site, the largest building at 46,000 square feet, which raised the budget for the project to approximately $260 million. Complex engineering was also needed to build the square over the railway lines that continue to service the nearby station. Developed with UK-based engineers Atelier One, a structural platform was constructed, decked over the railway lines and implanted with thousands of high-tensile springs. The concrete slab of

the square rests on top with the springs acting to dissipate the vibrations from the railway below.

The civic plaza is the connective tissue tying together the various buildings. Surfaced in sandstone, with demarcated grassy areas, the landscape of the plaza is made from a continuously folded surface that ramps up an entire story from the entrance at the northwest corner in front of the station, adjacent cathedral and new visitor center. The sandstone ranges in color from red, orange, and yellow to purple and mauve, giving it a distinctive character from the city's paving stones, and is inset with artworks by Paul Carter. The angular form of the plaza allows for a series of spaces accommodating larger gatherings as well as more intimate areas for relaxation, bordered by places to eat and drink. At the southwest of the site is an outdoor amphitheater with a stage designed to host music festivals and other large events. In 2003 it was the scene of an anti-war demonstration attended by more than 10,000 people. The stepped seating also functions as an auditorium to watch projections on the large video screen embedded into the façade of the pub located on the adjacent corner of the square. Envisioned as a display screen for digital art works and films, during the World Cup in 2002 major football games were shown to crowds of thousands.

The other key public space is a 65-foot-wide and 52-foot-high atrium made from a glass and steel honeycomb-like structure, hollow on the inside, which connects the plaza with the riverside promenade to the south. Open, with sliding doors at the east and west ends, the atrium is accessible by the public 24 hours a day. The soaring space acts as an additional concert venue with 50 percent given over to a stepped auditorium for music and theatre ensembles with an acoustically tuned interior. The building engages a passive cooling system that tempers the environment by way of a 130-square-foot concrete labyrinth positioned beneath the plaza and above the structural deck.

OUTLOOK

Federation Square is the first space of its kind in Melbourne. Intended to be part of the urban fabric, the square joins disparate parts of the city and helps animate the waterfront. Passageways carved between buildings and the predominance of glass allows for transparency giving new sightlines through the city and prompting new relationships with the urban landscape.

Aerial view of Federation Square,
Melbourne, Australia

PHOTO: © JOHN GOLLINGS

*Night view of Federation Square
on New Year's Eve 2002*

PHOTO: © PETER CLARKE

"By designing an environment that allows relationships to play out in complex scenarios, architects can encourage something dynamic: the emergence of a new city precinct that will generate its own continuous energies and habits. All the people and all the related material elements might start to behave like a complex system."

ROSS GIBSON,
POL OXYGEN MAGAZINE

"The opportunity to design Federation Square and have it built has been an almost six-year odyssey of intense research, experimentation, political confrontation, public denunciation, late nights, endless meetings, stupid design/construction interference, glorious collaborations, surprise, despair, and optimism, all propelled forward by the efforts of talented, dedicated individuals aspiring to the creation of an architecture of lasting importance."

DONALD BATES,
LAB ARCHITECTURE STUDIO

CITY HALL

OVERVIEW

The design of City Hall, by Foster and Partners, the new headquarters building of the Greater London Authority and home to the mayor's office, was driven by the idea of a "transparent government." The iconic structure, illuminated at night, is a new landmark for London with its internal workings visible to all. Exemplified through the structure of the building, the public can not only see in and view the workings of the mayor's office through the glazed façade but can enter the first two floors of the building for free during office hours (8am to 8pm) and on set weekends walk right to the top. (Dates and times are given at www.london.gov.uk.) In addition, all meetings of the Mayor's Advisory Committee and the London Assembly and its Committees, including the monthly Mayor's Question Time are open to the public. These are either held in the Chamber, which is located at the heart of the building or in one of the meetings rooms on the lower level.

DESIGNERS

Foster and Partners, led by Norman Foster and Spencer de Grey, David Nelson, Ken Shuttleworth and Graham Phillips, has established an international reputation with projects incorporating major public functions and spaces such as the new German Parliament in the Reichstag, Berlin, The Great Court for the British Museum, London, the Metro Bilbao, and the Carré d'Art, Nimes.

DESCRIPTION

City Hall is situated on the banks of the River Thames between London Bridge and Tower Bridge in an area recently named More London. The building forms part of a mixed-use development planned by Foster and Partners in 1998, after the firm won the developer/architect competition with the CIT Group, organized by the Labor government. The 13.6-acre site, which will include four additional office towers, a hotel, shops and cafés, all designed by Foster and Partners, had been largely abandoned in the 1980s. The site is accessible 24 hours a day by a wide footpath that links to London Bridge Station. A new service road underground shared by all the new buildings allows the entire site to be kept free of vehicles with more than half of the area given over to public space.

City Hall has both interior and exterior public gathering spaces that are free of charge. Given heightened security concerns, metal detectors at the entrances and CCTV cameras throughout the building monitor activity. However, these precautions are no more intrusive than the proliferation of CCTV cameras hung on every street corner in London.

The approximately 148-foot-high and 201,600-square-foot building is entered either through the ground level lobby or via a large sunken amphitheatre, which leads to a public café at the lower ground level. These entrances service both the staff and the public as does the café, further emphasizing the goal of the building to foster interaction among those inside and out. The restaurant spills out onto the 1,000-seat amphitheatre in the summer.

The lower level also contains meeting rooms and an exhibition space with a 1:1250 scale model of central London. From here a steel and concrete ramp, half a mile long and 92 feet high, coils up all ten stories. During the week the public can climb to the second floor and take in views over the city through the glass façade and also observe the lower level offices. On set weekends the entire ramp is open, which takes visitors through the Assembly Chamber, above the main debating chamber, and past the Mayor's office. At every level, views over London can be observed. At the top of the building is "London's Living Room," a 7,000 square-foot indoor and outdoor gallery and terrace with 330° views. Flooded with light, this space can accommodate 200, and is used for press conferences, exhibitions and conferences.

The iconic form of the building was determined by its environmental requirements to minimize heat gain and loss and maintain transparency. Foster, in conjunction with engineering firm Arup, predetermined that a geometric sphere, made from a framework of individually shaped glazed panels, would enable the building to achieve the greatest volume with the least surface area. To the south, the building steps back; floors overhang one another, shading the level below. City Hall succeeds in consuming 75% less energy than equivalent high-rise office towers.

OUTLOOK

The Reichstag in Berlin, Foster and Partners' first government building to experiment with transparency, allows the public to enter the building and walk up inside a double-helix ramp cone to the dome at the very top. City Hall symbolically expands on this idea by giving the public greater access to and views of the workings of the democratic process, which is made visible at night when the building is illuminated.

View of City Hall, London, United Kingdom, on the River Thames

PHOTO: © NIGEL YOUNG/ FOSTER AND PARTNERS

Interior view of City Hall's public ramp, looking up

PHOTO: © NIGEL YOUNG/ FOSTER AND PARTNERS

"Our goal was to make a building that was as open and as accessible as possible. People walking by can look in and see committee meetings taking place. Once inside, the public can walk from London's Living Room at the top, down through the Assembly Chamber, and past the mayor's office, and view the workings of City Hall."

MAX NEAL, PROJECT DIRECTOR, FOSTER AND PARTNERS

PONTE PARODI

OVERVIEW

In May 2001, UN Studio won an international competition to design the Ponte Parodi in Genoa's harbor, an almost 6-acre pier. The project, on a 19th-century pier whose 20th-century grain towers had become redundant, was to be the linchpin in transforming Genoa's historic port from its industrial era into one that still made use of the water—as a terminal for ferries and cruise ships—but put in the context of a leisure-driven urban core, that would attract residents, students, and tourists. The reuse of the 1886 breakwater, which was named after its engineer Adolfo Parodi and holds the status of the most important monument of the early industrialization of Genoa's port, is a potent symbol for a new urban life in the 21st century.

DESIGNER

UN Studio's breakthrough waterfront project was the Erasmus Bridge, in Rotterdam, opened in 1996, which integrated principals Ben van Berkel and Caroline Bos's ongoing preoccupations with designs that are "kaleidoscopic" in their conceptualization, offering an infinite series of surfaces and spaces, resisting coming to rest in a singular perspective or section, and thus incorporating their conception of the circular flow of contemporary life. And despite their protestations against designing icons, the visual impact of its colossal wishbone pylon in pale blue is a visually unforgettable addition to its city's public realm. The Ponte Parodi, even as it takes on hundreds of thousands of square feet of activity as it strives to create a 24/7 version of Italian city life, is likely to be equally arresting.

DESCRIPTION

The three-dimensional "piazza sul mediterraneo" is vast in area and volume, requiring scores of programs, ranging from interior and exterior areas for sports, exhibitions, movie theaters, discos, retail, restaurants, media studios, an auditorium, and offices. To encompass this, the designers envisioned a colossal cube, and pulled it apart to accommodate the need for multiple levels, access, and key public spaces that could lead visitors through the program. The result is two principal public spaces: the hilltop, whose form echoes the hills surrounding the harbor, and is occupied by sports and passive recreation, and the wharf-level piazza, which accommodates the crowds of passenger ship tourists debarking, as well as the largest flows of visitors from the city, coming for the full program of recreation that the pier offers.

Thus, the piazza is hardly historic in character, carved out of its synthetic hill in the harbor, but it is deliberately connected to the city's history by its views both to Genoa and to the Mediterranean, all calculated as part of an intense calculus of time, site and climate-specific "program finders" that could lead visitors to and through the four main "program clusters" of the project: entertainment, wellness, technology, commerce, and the ship terminal functions. In short, in a thoroughly contemporary idiom, UN Studio has sought to provide the pleasures of a Mediterranean city's public spaces—morning coffee in the sun, midday shopping in the shade, and evening socializing with a view of the sunset. They have also imagined this with a provocatively contemporary program, including a huge factory outlet center, seen as an attractor for residents, and as part of a strategy for the Ponte Parodi to be an economically viable, mixed-use location.

OUTLOOK

UN Studio has looked to Venice's Piazza San Marco as an inspiration—a piazza that captured the public's imagination for generations, for many of which it had a clear set of civic functions and rituals beyond accommodating pigeons and tourists in its cafes. An Italian piazza without religion or government, and with a factory outlet center, may be the embodiment of the 21st century, but like many other contemporary public spaces, it faces the challenge of being a space entirely untethered to overt public activities. In addition, while it does have an infrastructural function, serving ship passengers, it will, like several other waterfront sites, face the challenge of generating the aura of a "crossroads" for multiple functions and publics. The project's power is in a design created to overcome these inherent challenges, which, as much as the new waterfront functions themselves, will create what van Berkel has called the "piazza effect" where a place is not just space to go through, but to come to and use.

Aerial view of Ponte Parodi, a mixed-use terminal for ferries and recreational activities

"The principal requirement in the competition program was for a square by the sea: a square Genoa has never had but now shall, surrounded by the sea on three sides...It should be added...that we are dealing with a scheme that will have to meet the costs of realization and operation: in a word, one that has to make a profit."

BRUNO GABRIELLI,
GENO(V)A: DEVELOPING AND REBOOTING A WATERFRONT CITY (NAI)

"Globalization, often equated with Americanization, is seen as seriously eroding local culture and cohesiveness, substituting a generic brand identity...The challenge for Genoa, then, is to invest the new leisure destination over the Ponte Parodi with an architectural and interpersonal brio that conveys the city's unique independent spirit and sense of modernity."

JOHN HANNIGAN,
GENO(V)A: DEVELOPING AND REBOOTING A WATERFRONT CITY (NAI)

TIANANMEN, TRAFALGAR, AND THE ABIDING IMPERTINENCE OF PUBLIC SPACE

Deyan Sudjic is the architecture critic of the *The Observer*, in London. He is a former editor of *Domus* magazine in Milan, and was director of the Venice Architecture Biennale in 2002. He is currently writing a book on architecture and power

For those who still regard the concept of public space as no more than a sugary, nebulous and ultimately sentimental idea of the city, a kind of cosmetic representation of place defined in terms of more or less elegant park benches, customized street lights, unnecessarily emphatic paving, and an endless proliferation of signage, I would recommend a trip to Beijing. It's a metropolis of 14 million people that is giving Houston and Los Angeles a salutary lesson in what tooth and claw, laissez-faire planning, or rather no planning, really means, and which provides a timely reminder of what urban space is actually about, if only because of its complete absence.

Beijing celebrates the 850th anniversary of its foundation this year as an imperial city built to guard China's northern frontiers, and designed as a physical representation of the universe. And on one level, that is the most meaningful kind of public space imaginable, even if it had nothing that could be called a piazza, or a plaza, the archetypes that have kept western architectural imaginations in thrall. For the first 800 years of its existence, Beijing retained essentially the same character, the walled palace inner city at its center, organized on a strict north-south axis, contained within a sea of courtyard houses, the hutongs, with lanes too narrow for motor traffic, and rarely even the most rudimentary sanitation. For the last ten years, Beijing has turned into the largest construction site that the world has ever seen, a frenetic exercise in *tabula rasa* development, as both traditional neighborhoods and the monuments of the Mao era are demolished to make way for office towers, hotels and shopping malls.

Mao declared the People's Republic from the Gate of Heavenly Peace, looking out over the newly paved Tiananmen Square where park benches were few and far between. With the help of his Soviet ally, he attempted to turn the city into the center of a modern China, but the imperial structure remained unchanged. Tiananmen with its vast parade ground, a hint of what Hitler and Speer would have done to Berlin, was the symbol of the new order, but it was still aligned on the Forbidden City. The communist monuments built around it were larger and more imposing than those of the emperors, but they also laid claim to them. Urban space was being used to project an unmistakable political message just as it had in the days of the emperors, even if the emphasis was rather different.

What appealed most to an authoritarian regime about Beijing was that the city had no urban tradition in the western sense. It was divided into self contained zones, its open spaces were ceremonial rather than public, offering less scope for the masses to develop minds of their own than the more democratic spaces of some European cities. The Chinese communist party accentuated the authoritarian characteristics of its capital. It divided Beijing into compounds—some reserved for industry, others for the universities, the army, the hospitals, and the embassies—and ensured that there was minimal communication between them. A big factory compound could house 10,000 people, offering them beds, canteens, and schools; ensuring that they could spend their entire lives within the perimeter wall. A city like this presents a minimal challenge to a ruling autocracy. There was no democratic space either in Mao's or in Imperial Beijing, no commercial area, no restaurants even. After 9pm the city seemed to shut down altogether, reduced, less than a decade ago, to medieval darkness. The city no longer goes dark. It is evolving in ways, which its rulers can no longer fully control. But it has not yet managed to find its own version of public space. It has adopted the shopping mall, but has eschewed the idea of democratic space. Within its chaotic state of constant change, some impulses tend to bring out the anarchic qualities that characterize an authentic city. And other, equally strong currents are pushing in the opposite direction. Immediately west of Tiananmen Square hundreds of courtyard houses have been flattened to build the National Opera house; a megalomaniac glass egg designed by Paul Andreu, a French architect specializing in airports with an unwholesome fondness for the work of Claude Nicolas Ledoux. His contribution to central Beijing's wide-open prairies is to put the opera house in the middle of a lake. It is the perfect contemporary face for a regime that believes in the use of tanks as a modern instrument of crowd control. Hanging baskets of flowers and granite pavements are not going to turn Beijing into the capital city of a liberal democracy. But the creation of a genuine public realm would be more than a purely symbolic gesture in this direction. Without it, Beijing will be the first metropolis to pass directly from a city with a feudal structure to the beltway anomie of an authoritarian version of Texas in which every vestige of public space has been privatized.

Contemporary space does not spring fully formed from nowhere. We make spaces in the first instance, just as we make buildings, to carry out their functional mission. And sometimes these buildings and these spaces become something else, an icon, or a landmark, a measure of life in the contemporary city.

London's most highly charged public space is Trafalgar Square; named for imperial Britain's crucial victory over the Napoleonic fleet, and dominated by the bizarre surrealism of a gigantic Corinthian column topped by a larger than life representation of Horatio Nelson, the naval hero of the wars with the French. The form of the square is the product of a series of pragmatic decisions made as the result of John Nash's transformation of random fragments of London at the beginning of the 19th century into a modern metropolis. It is where Britain's radicals gathered to protest at the oppressive policies of its 19th-century governments, with regular loss of life when the military used violence to suppress demonstrations. It is where the anti-apartheid movement kept up a constant vigil outside the embassy of the white-ruled South Africa, an action that according to Nelson Mandela (and the choice of first name says a lot in these particular circumstances) played an important part in the peaceful transition of his country to majority rule. The square is where the giant anti-nuclear demonstrations of the 1960s had their culminating rallies. But it is also where revelers gather to celebrate New Year's Eve. Trafalgar Square is like Washington's Mall and Times Square rolled into one, both a symbolic and social center for urban life. It has also been a notoriously problematic space, reduced to an island cut off by heavy traffic from the city around it. Its current incarnation is the product of Norman Foster's restructuring, the biggest transformation of the square since the start of World War II when Edwin Landseer Lutyens installed the fountains.

One of the great myths about London is that it is a city with no tradition of planning in the grand manner. In fact it was Napoleon III's exile, when he saw for himself John Nash's heroic urban surgery from Regents Park all the way to Westminster that was eventually to trigger his attempt to do the same in Paris. Nash created some of the great set pieces that still give London its character—the palatial terraces of the park, Regent Street, Piccadilly Circus. And of course Trafalgar Square itself.

When Nash turned his attention to the area, the only landmark that still survived was James Gibb's sublime baroque church of St Martins-in-the-Fields, finished in 1726. But it was hemmed in by meanly proportioned houses, and flanked by the royal stables. Nash saw this as a crucial road junction, at the meeting point of the east west route from the City of London to the West End, and the north south route linking it to Westminster, a dilemma that is familiar to every expanding city today. Nash suggested a square, flanked by suitable major public buildings. Demolitions began in 1824—creating the setting for the church that Foster's closure of the road on the north side of the square now enhances. On the west side, Robert Smirke built the Royal College of Physicians that is now Canada House. On the north side is the National Gallery, designed by William Wilkins. In the next century, many of Britain's most distinguished architects worked in and around the square. Charles Barry dealt with the disconcerting slope of the square in 1840 when he created the ledge in front of the National Gallery, and two flights of steps down into the square on either side. Nelson's column was erected in 1842. Edwin Landseer carved the lions in 1868. Aston Webb designed the Admiralty Arch in 1906. Herbert Baker built South Africa House in 1935 on the east side, and Edwin Lutyens designed the fountains, his last commission, in 1939. Finally, Robert Venturi and Denise Scott Brown built the Sainsbury wing of the National Gallery. There are curious parallels between John Nash, the architect of regency London and Norman Foster. Both have turned out to be prolific architects, to the extent that their critics and their peers began to question their ability to build well. And both were architects who ended up as interested in remodeling London, as in the design of any individual building. Foster has spent five years working on the square.

Despite the impressive collection of architectural talent that has engaged with it over the last two centuries, it has sometimes been hard to love the results. There are the feral pigeons; now a little thinner on the ground after Mayor Ken Livingstone's offensive against them, there is the noisome traffic and the frankly unsatisfactory nature of the architectural centerpiece, the National Gallery, with its tentative and inconclusive facade, and its uncomfortably perfunctory central dome. Worse still is the curiously cut off nature of the square itself. It may fill to capacity for a major demonstration or a New Year's Eve celebration but in the everyday course of events, it is the last place bonafide Londoners are likely to find themselves, even on a sunny June afternoon, let alone a cold and wet winter's day. It has, until now been glimpsed from the tops of busses, or cut off not just by traffic but also by the low walls that line three sides. Foster has worked long and hard to rescue the square from its most obvious shortcomings. He has managed to persuade the authorities to close the north side to traffic, connected the national gallery with the square with a dramatic new flight of steps, and resurfaced much of the resulting pedestrian space.

It is true that the square would be a better place with no traffic at all, or perhaps just red buses. But the strip at the north is worth having. The pavement in front of the National Gallery used to be as crammed, and as vertiginous as the platform on the subway line at Leicester Square. Now it is an open space that stretches smoothly over the lip of the square, and is linked to it by what will no doubt become one of the great places to sit out doors in London. These are a set of flights of steps on a truly architectural scale, London's answer to St. Petersburg's Nevsky Prospect. It is a great place to look out over the square, and down to Whitehall beyond. But it also does something to overcome the weakness of the National Gallery's facade, by giving its center section the appearance of a thicker base, it gives it a less horizontal emphasis.

Foster's treatment of the stairs is respectful to a fault. He has cut through the back wall in a way that makes you think that nothing has happened. The detail is 19th century, except for the two glass lifts for the disabled. And he has created a number of quiet, but monumental interventions, bronze and granite steps, and benches that have a timeless monumentality. Foster's creation of London's new City Hall, to house the newly reconstituted administration of the mayor, has done its best to create a space with the urban qualities and political resonance of Trafalgar Square. City Hall's public space is a spiral auditorium that echoes the corkscrew atrium at the heart of the building. Handsome though it is, this New Year's Eve, it is still not going to be a challenge to Trafalgar Square as a gathering place for London revelers.

Melbourne, set beside either Beijing, or London is a young city, established in the 19th century, laid out by a surveyor's grid sent site unseen from London, driven by a gold rush. The new Federation Square, created by Lab Architecture Studio, represents an intriguing attempt to create a public space that mediates between an urban structure shaped by classical European precedents, in an entirely new context, and at the same time attempts to show that urban space can lead the growth of a city, as well as follow. Federation Square is both an architectural and an urban intervention; a collection of cultural buildings, arrayed around artificial ground created by bridging the railway tracks leading to Melbourne's main railway station that has had the effect of cutting the city in two. Lab's work combines architecture with landscape in a single vision to give Melbourne a space that is both a link and a central focus, adopting a range of architectural expressions that are both rooted in traditional ideas of public space, and expressed in contemporary terms.

It is possible to travel the world, and discover examples of new attempts at creating public space everywhere, from Foster's work in Trafalgar Square, and also his City Hall in London, and Lab in Melbourne, in UN Studio's waterfront for Genoa, in the work of West 8 in Rotterdam, and many others. The vitality of much of this work is a reminder of the continuing contemporary relevance of public space, one of the oldest conceptions of urbanism, and its abiding importance.

OPENING THE CITY

In the last four decades' reaction against the destructive impact of highways on cities' fabrics of communities, it was sometimes forgotten that the transportation infrastructure for moving people and goods is the lifeblood of a city, and that even the most egregiously intrusive can be reconceived as benign, or at least less malignant, public space. Different continents and different economies may call for different solutions, but there is no excuse for condemning citizens, car-owners or not, to a city of dangerous streets, broken sidewalks and second-rate transit.

In **Bogotá, Columbia,** a forceful mayor with a vision of social and environmental justice pushed through a system of boulevards that excluded motorized vehicles. The Alamedas are for walkers and bicyclists, connecting neighborhoods of different incomes and different levels of development. Since their opening, they have been used by a broad range of city dwellers, from those who choose to ride a bicycle for health and convenience, to those for whom exercise is a necessity, not a choice. In **Rio de Janeiro, Brazil,** key new streets, for both pedestrians and emergency vehicles, have opened the favelas (the informal and originally illegal hillside settlements) to city services. Completed or underway in 20 favelas, the typical project connects the district to the rest of Rio, and the literal physical connection is supplemented by new public spaces and programs. These are carved out of the existing neighborhood with a minimum of razed buildings, and only after community review. In **Macon, Georgia,** the stretch of Poplar Street that once fronted the old cotton warehouses had declined for decades into a place you drove through without stopping, with a scraggly median down the middle of its almost two-hundred-foot width. The city decided that while the roadway still had to serve as a county highway, a design for the street—not a storefront improvements campaign, but in the roadbed—could change that. When completed, the design will give the broad street a series of squares, with easy parking on the sides and middle, and a generous planted median. The strategy is to recognize that the social give-and-take of a parking lot—with some shade—would make a real connection to both local history and to the way people live and work today. Changing scale, in **London, United Kingdom,** a major arterial running four miles through neighborhoods and industrial districts was reconceived through design interventions, from an unforgettable field of light poles to new and reconsidered pedestrian and bike paths, as well as plantings and structures between road and the boroughs. Cities have been nearly undone by roadways that literally and metaphorically have left people behind, while these new projects take the opposite direction.

POPLAR STREET

OVERVIEW

The 180-foot-wide boulevard in the center of Macon, Georgia, 75 miles southeast of Atlanta, called for urban regeneration, bordered as it was by vacant storefronts and empty sidewalks. The response, part of the larger Macon-Bibb County Road Improvement project, is about changing a road's purpose from servicing through traffic to making a sequence of public spaces. The Mayors Institute of City Design and the National Endowment for the Arts worked with the Mayor of Macon to develop a design competition that would break with the standard storefront and sidewalk improvements approach.

DESIGNER

Walter Hood's distinct way of changing urban landscapes is an interactive process of outreach to the community through his visual and verbal narratives, often illustrated as in his "Urban Diaries," connecting the site and its clients to his own thought process. He is skeptical of relying on standard review processes, in which the designer is reduced to the role of either recording secretary or cornered into being a defiant artiste, and strives instead to combine an intuitive and analytical approach combined with historical research into how people used a place in the past, and how they really might use it in the future, from the mean streets of the urban fringe to well-funded gardens adjacent to a major art museum.

DESCRIPTION

Poplar Street was never Main Street, but with City Hall only a block away, and a major church at the top of its slope, it was always at the heart of Macon's downtown. The Macon Yards project is located where the city's most important historic trade—cotton—was once brought to blocks of warehouses, and the 150-foot curb-to-curb roadway's width comes from a time when it had to support the crush of traffic moving the cotton in and out. In terms of geography, the site has a more than thirty-foot drop—this really is the edge of the flatlands, the furthest inland that you could navigate upriver.

In the late 1990s, the design team worked to uncover the site's layers of identity, from geology to the recent past. Macon was the home, and musical hometown, for artists including Lena Horne and Little Richard, in a music scene that thrived into the 1960s. Yet for the team, the site wasn't wearing history on its sleeve—the roadway had a few scraggly plantings in a narrow median, lots of lanes, and not much memory of what had happened there or nearby.

In response, they navigated between public and private histories, and landed on the concept of "yards," inspired by very different southern landscapes, from the swept dirt yards of African-Americans' past to the "squares" devised for English settlements in Savannah and Charleston. The yards are integrated into an overall division of the street, 50 feet for cars, 50 feet for median, 50 feet for cars, and each Yard is about 150-foot square. When finished, their surface will be in the earth-hues of local aggregate, rather than black asphalt (the idea of swept yards's hard-packed dirt never had much of a chance with traffic engineers). In the center third there are a markets, water running down to the coastal plain, shade trees, and historic markers, but most of all, the Yards will perform as parking lots. In Macon, everybody drives everywhere, Hood observes, and in the Yards, drivers and pedestrians will share the space.

OUTLOOK

Combining the function of roadway and public space, and proposing a new idea to a public sector where elected officials and community attitudes change over time, is inevitably challenging, but when completed it will be a critical demonstration of how to reinvent rather than romanticize urban public space.

View of Poplar Street, Macon, Georgia, looking northeast, showing urban improvements

RENDERING: HOOD DESIGN

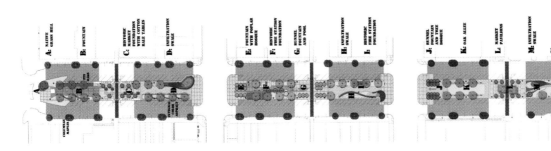

Plan of Poplar Street

PLAN: HOOD DESIGN

"When applied to urban planning and design, improvisation—in its generic meaning, creating, fabricating, and composing and using what is at hand—is a method of reshaping a particular environment based on preexisting local resources, inspirations, and opportunities."

WALTER HOOD,
"URBAN DIARIES," IN *EVERYDAY URBANISM* (THE MONACELLI PRESS)

The Macon design is based on "caring about what people say, what people want, and what people have done to the place over time."

WALTER HOOD,
HOOD DESIGN

FAVELA-BAIRRO PROJECT

RIO DE JANEIRO, BRAZIL
JÁUREGUI ARCHITECTS

OVERVIEW

Rio de Janeiro's favelas (shantytowns) house a fourth of the city's population. Approximately 1,500,000 people, in a city of six million, live in these unplanned communities that began to emerge over 100 years ago. Developing organically, today they are dense neighborhoods of ramshackle housing made from simple materials that are primarily located on the steep slopes of the mountains overlooking the city and the Atlantic Ocean. Set apart from the rest of Rio, these neighborhoods are without street names and numbers, literally unmapped territories lacking an official identity. They are prone to landslides caused by rainfall, lack of drainage, formal services, and are often only accessible by steep footpaths.

DESIGNERS/SPONSORS

The "Favela-Bairro Project," under the auspices of the City of Rio's "Urban Scheme," is a nine-year project, begun in 1995, prompted by the 1993 Housing Policy, an addendum to the 1992 city Master Plan. The primary goal is the integration of the favelas with the rest of the city, the provision of services, and the facilitation of community interaction. Jáuregui Architects, based in Rio and headed by Jorge Mario Jáuregui, won the government-initiated open competition in 1995 and has since designed and developed over 20 favelas, including the Fernão Cardim, Fubá-Campinho, Rio das Pedras and Macacos. The firm has since gone on to develop similar projects in Argentina, Venzuela, and Chile.

PROCESS

The project is based on three main approaches to urban renewal: physical, social, and psychological. Rather than eradicating existing neighborhoods or a series of assistance programs (conventional failed approaches undertaken since the 1930s), the Favela-Bairro project hinges on the potential of the existing favelas and their inhabitants to create vital and healthy communities through a number of multiple scale interventions. The involvement of the residents through public forums enable the local community to interact with Jáuregui's multidisciplinary team of architects, engineers, planners, sociologists, psychiatrists, educators, medical personnel, and social workers. They also have final say on whether a project is approved.

DESCRIPTION

Jáuregui's scheme is focused on integrating the favelas with the rest of the city. The first strategy is delineating roads and pedestrian routes to link existing circulation paths at the exterior of the favelas with those on the interior. These pathways allow water, power, sewers, communications, and the police to enter the favelas, which were previously controlled by drug traffickers. In the case of the Fubá-Campinho, two favelas of approximately 3,500 families that were linked together in 2000 as part of the Favela-Bairro Project, new roads and pathways solved a waste disposal problem. Before the roads, there were no designated drop-off points for garbage collection. The creation of public spaces such as the central square at the heart of the Macacos favela, has created a community gathering area. Other facilities are integrated within the favelas such as a community center, laundry, a samba school, or soccer field. In the Rio das Pedras favela, with a population of 60,000 (12,000 families), there is a new health care center, and a skateboarding park. Often these improvements are located at the boundaries to further integrate the city and the favela.

The projects, which integrate design strategies of bold colors and signage, are planned to offer long-term benefits to the community. Much of the construction can be done by unskilled labor and people who live in the favelas are employed, receiving job training, and the skills to maintain the favelas after the project is completed.

OUTLOOK

Jáuregui's integrated approach is a model of sustainable development for Rio's favelas that has not only upgraded and introduced much needed services and facilities but has proven key to an inclusive approach to generating interactivity amongst residents and a sense of pride and belonging. The program is a reminder that the design of public spaces can be effectively integrated with a broader program.

View of service building in the Macacos favela, Rio de Janiero, Brazil

PHOTO: GABRIEL LEANDRO JÁUREGUI

Aerial view of the Campinho favela, Rio de Janeiro, Brazil, showing new soccer field and community buildings

PHOTO: GABRIEL LEANDRO JÁUREGUI

"Until recently the favelas have been Rio's invisible city —uncharted, literally off the map...The aim of the Favela-Bairro Project is to make these formerly alienated areas an integral part of the city."

ELIZABETH MOSSOP, ASSOCIATE PROFESSOR, HARVARD DESIGN SCHOOL

"The Favela-Bairro aims to produce what we might call 'urban excitement' by pointing out the qualities, the potentialities and the level of integration hoped for in the public spaces."

JORGE MARIO JÁUREGUI, JÁUREGUI ARCHITECTS

ARTSCAPE, A13

OVERVIEW

In the most extensive public art project ever funded in England, architect Tom de Paor has developed a master plan for a series of art works that punctuate an almost four-mile stretch of the A13 highway, which links London to the East Coast. The A13 Artscape is an effort to bring a new reading to the industrial landscape of the highway, which passes through the London Borough of Barking and Dagenham. 60,000 cars a day travel through this section of the A13, which is also partly bordered by houses, schools and recreation areas. The project aims to portray an identity for Barking and Dagenham and prompt drivers with visual stimuli as they pass through two discrete districts.

Large-scale landscapes, light works, sculpture and street furniture are some of the schemes for the road, which were developed as part of a master plan in 1996, which has funding from the National Lottery and the Arts Council of England. The project is a ten-year initiative that takes advantage of already programmed road works by the Highways Agency that are part of an overarching initiative to regenerate the East Thames Gateway, an area along the north bank of the Thames between Docklands and the Greater London Boundary. The artworks have been incorporated into the edges of the highway and sometimes at more central points such as roundabouts and junctions in phases. Fifteen works in total are in various stages of completion, design development or being conceptualized with the plan that they will all be realized by 2006.

DESIGNER

Tom de Paor is principal of de Paor Architects based in Dublin, Ireland. His most recent achievements include winning Britain's Corus/Building Design Young Architect of the Year award in 2003. In 2000 he designed the Irish pavilion at the Venice Architecture Biennale. Other public projects include the Visitor Centre at Ballincollig County Cork that he designed with Emma O'Neill in 1991.

DESCRIPTION

De Paor was chosen through an invited selection process in 1996. He views the project as an urban strategy for a linear park along the edge of the highway in which repeated elements are interposed with larger scale objects and sculptures. More subtle interventions such as the planting of trees along a mile stretch of the road, intercepted by bespoke cast iron grills (providing an acoustic barrier for the nearby housing estate) are accompanied by more dramatic designs that cut into the fabric of the surrounding landscape. For example, a half-mile long, straight pathway made from gold, white and green tarmac, currently in design development, will bisect a flat section of land and connect pedestrians and cyclists to playing fields and a children's playground and keep people away from the road. Other smaller scale strategies include reconsidering and reinterpreting standard civil engineering components to create interesting new visual effects such as using glass bead reflective white paint on sculptures to reflect the headlights of passing vehicles instead of standard roadway paint. The largest project, "Holding Pattern," is the first large-scale work to be completed. Unveiled in 2000, the permanent installation was a collaboration with artists Graham Ellard and Stephen Johnstone, realized with funds from the Arts Lottery, Single Regeneration Budget, European Union, and private funding. Twenty-six eighteen-foot-high, by four-inch diameter stainless steel light columns, each tipped with a blue airport taxiway light, illuminate the Lodge Avenue roundabout. Arranged in a grid, the datum for the lights corresponds to the height of the existing metal flyover that crosses the roundabout. Drivers reach the plateau of the lights only when they reach the top of the flyover. From the ground as drivers circle the roundabout, the columns act as a rotating disc of light. By day the columns act as a field of polished needles filtering views across the highway. In addition, de Paor is developing a number of designs that have been inspired by the area's history. A series of three 98-foot-high towers made from oak are being designed to delineate the original edge of the Thames northern floodplain and will also act as orientation points for drivers.

OUTLOOK

Highways are not typically thought of as sites for public art, yet de Paor's Artscape project is not only of visual interest but increases safety, defines pathways for pedestrians and cyclists and provides an additional light source. The project is also used by London City Airport as a navigational device. By working with the Highways Agency at the beginning of their road works project, de Paor was able to build his designs into their plans, which reduces costs and ensures the art works become an integral feature of the highway. An opportunity to rethink a challenging site, the Artscape project has redefined Barking and Dagenham's identity and has placed them on the cultural map.

Night view of Holding Pattern, a lighting design installed along the A13 highway, London, United Kingdom

PHOTO: DOUGLAS ATFIELD

View of Landscaping along the A13 highway

PHOTO: DOUGLAS ATFIELD

"The project was conceived to enhance the A13 and lift the awareness of the motorist from the bleak industrial landscape with extraordinary space and features that are unapologetic in their strong sense of artistic design."

TRACEY MCNULTY,
LONDON BOROUGH OF BARKING AND DAGENHAM

"The project was an opportunity to rethink a place and a landscape with a series of choreographed elements."

TOM DE PAOR, DE PAOR ARCHITECTS

ALAMEDA EL PORVENIR

BOGOTÁ, COLOMBIA
MGP ARQUITECTURA Y URBANISMO

OVERVIEW

In the last hundred years, Bogotá in central Colombia, a city 8,500 feet above sea level, has gone from a population of 105,000 to seven million inhabitants. Rapid densification and the informal development of the city's core, predominantly based on illegal housing schemes that preclude proper services such as sewage disposal, electricity and schools and health centers, coupled with poor city roads and mass transit obliging residents to rely on cars or sustain lengthy commutes, have prompted the city to take action.

Following a variety of incremental measures, the city passed Law 338 in 1997, which stipulated a ten-year master plan for urban redevelopment.

SPONSORS/DESIGNERS

"The Plan de Ordenamiento Territorial" or POT (Territory Regulating Plan for Bogotá) was designed under the leadership of Mayor Enrique Peñalosa Londoño (1997-2001). His plan was four-fold involving: recovering public spaces for pedestrian and bicycle activities; introducing new and regulating existing services; constructing a more efficient and environmentally safe transportation system; and providing land for low-income housing. Key to Peñalosa's vision was fostering equality and imbuing citizens with a sense of pride and belonging, and a long-term vision for radically reducing automobile use.

POT defined public space as the main tool to achieving the above goals. The plan sought to create a network of high quality public spaces, by introducing strategies for clearing sidewalks of carparks, recovering existing green spaces or through more ambitious schemes such as the Red de Alamedas (Alameda Net for Bogotá), the pilot project for the Alameda El Porvenir.

The Municipal Urban Design Office overseeing the project reached out to the city's architects, recognizing the need for designers who could rise to the challenge and utilize a multi-disciplinary approach, not only planning or engineering. In 1997 they hired MGP arquitectura y urbanismo, a firm based in Bogotá and specializing in public projects, headed by Felipe Gonzalez-Pacheco and Juan Ignacio Munoz-Tamayo.

DESCRIPTION

The Alameda El Porvenir was defined as an approximately 11-mile green network of pedestrian and cycle paths carved through the southwest part of Bogotá, an area of low-income and unregulated development. As well as generating safe and pleasant recreational areas, the boulevards were envisioned as an additional connector in Peñalosa's comprehensive city plan, providing residents with a transportation system that connects with adjacent neighborhoods, new schools, parks and libraries and the Transmilenio bus network, an improved system that runs on a dedicated roadway around the city, parallel to the other traffic.

MGP devised a three phase plan: the first was the establishment of an overall master plan, delineating the routes and negotiating technical and legal issues. The second was outlining the nature of the pathways, locating areas for larger gathering spaces and other public areas and finalizing a construction plan and timeline. The third was designing a repeatable, flexible system of public spaces that could be inserted into the promenade at intervals and constructed in a very short time frame. The initial four miles were scheduled to be finished in 15 months with a budget of $643,700 per mile.

The Alameda El Porvenir is characterized by a 92-foot wide pathway, divided into three strips: one for bikes; a median lined with palm trees and other plantings, with intermittent street furniture and lighting and; another for pedestrians. At points along the route, interstitial public spaces provide both small gathering areas with benches and simple sheltering devices such as screens and more extensive open areas for recreational activities and events.

OUTLOOK

The Alameda as it has been constructed passes through existing neighborhoods as well as land that has not yet been built. The project provides a unique opportunity to stimulate urban regeneration as well as integrate the alamedas from the start, encouraging sustainable development and better living conditions in the future.

View of Alameda El Porvenir, Bogotá, Colombia

MGP ARQUITECTURA Y URBANISMO

Aerial Plan of the Alameda El Porvenir showing the 11 mile green network of pedestrian and cycle paths

PHOTO: FOTO RUDOLF, COLOMBIA

"At our first meeting, the mayor decided to walk the 11 miles of the proposed route of the Alameda. It gave us a detailed idea of what he was thinking the Alameda should be. We also understood his commitment to the city. This was a vital motivation for us."

FELIPE GONZÁLEZ-PACHECO, MGP ARQUITECTURA Y URBANISMO

"High quality public spaces bring people out. Safety increases; people enjoy their city and acquire a sense of belonging. More than sidewalks or bicycle paths, we built symbols of equality and respect for human dignity."

ENRIQUE PEÑALOSA LONDOÑO, FORMER MAYOR OF BOGOTÁ

MOVEMENT
AND
PUBLIC SPACE

Elizabeth Mossop is a
landscape architect and
an Associate Professor at
Harvard Design School

Infrastructure increasingly provides the public spaces of our cities and the infrastructure of movement is an essential presence. It is the connection of elements to one another that provides the foundation of urban and suburban life. Like other infrastructure, roads are required to perform multiple functions and this is driving new design approaches. They have to fulfill the requirements of public space and they have to be connected to other functioning urban systems of public transit, pedestrian movement, water management, economic development, public facilities and ecological systems. The projects discussed here allow an examination of these issues through specific design investigations and the influence of context.

ROAD INFRASTRUCTURE AS SOCIAL NETWORK

The fundamental role of roads and pathways in urban life is expressed in the series of Favela-Bairro projects in Rio undertaken by Jauregui Architects where they have been used to make both a symbolic and a real transformation of these illegal settlements into a recognized part of the formal city. The roads and paths integrate the dwellers of these illegal settlements into the city proper and begin to provide them with basic services.

In this series of projects, the roads and walkways were carved from existing residential areas, which formed a continuous mat of illegally built housing, separated only by tiny walkways, without any means of getting any kind of vehicle through the area. The roads, as well as providing access, have made new public space where none existed before. They perform symbolic and physical functions of connection. They also allow the physical presence of the state, as police are able, for the first time, to physically move through the areas trying to control the organized crime and drug trafficking endemic in most of these areas. The new roads provide an artery for the distribution of basic services and they allow the creation of points of concentration for gathering and the location of public amenities. The naming and numbering of these roads also allows the extension of the city mapping into these areas for the first time and gives these dwellings a location and identity in the city as a whole, effectively giving them a reality they have not had before.

In the developed world particularly, road and highway projects are often the least constrained by financial considerations. The perception is that they are essential and that they must fulfill their engineering requirements and so they are immune from the modifications that accommodate other, non-traffic interests. For this reason, the surgical quality of these roads and walkways is very unusual in designs for new roads. A number of constraints forced an economy of strategy, resulting in configurations of the least action for the maximum impact. The very strict financial limits of the projects limited construction expenditure, the very strict social controls prevented the removal of more than 5% of the houses and very often, the extreme slopes of the favelas also constrained the form of roads and paths. So the form of the public space created by the roads is very precisely controlled. The location of new public facilities is an integral part of the network, and the associated gathering spaces serve very specific and many-layered functions.

THE PEOPLE'S ROAD

In Bogotá, the projects implemented during Mayor Peñalosa's administration aimed to create symbols of a more egalitarian city of democracy where there is the "prevalence of public good over private interest." A series of initiatives were undertaken to redress the historical privilege of the car-owning class, implementing projects that give primacy to pedestrian space, and facilitate alternative means of transport. They are particularly striking because they have physically removed space from use by private cars, parking spaces and lanes on the road, to implement projects for busways, and space for cyclists and pedestrians. The overt social and political aims of the strategy are given clear physical expression in the Alameda El Porvenir, designed by MGP Arquitectura y Urbanismo, which is a circulation spine for pedestrians and cyclists that connects into the new Transmilenio busway system.

Alameda means tree-lined promenade, and the Alameda El Porvenir provides a pedestrian route separated from a cycleway by a median planted with palms. Unusually the infrastructure has preceded the development. It links areas of development but is often traversing undeveloped areas and will sometimes be the first element developed in new neighborhoods. It passes through empty fields, past shanty towns, through new housing, and established neighborhoods. Its character varies dramatically, in some instances it is shaded by established trees, in others barren pavement is dotted with tiny palms. It is designed to perform more than just transit functions, incorporating gathering spaces, planting, and seating areas. Even in its rather undeveloped state, without mature planting and often passing through areas without development, it is animated by walkers, cyclists, dogs, food vendors, market stalls, skaters and joggers. In the informally developed neighborhoods that it passes through, it creates the only public space in these areas, which do not have paved roads or other facilities and services.

The actual road design is constrained by a limited budget, the cross section, materials and detailing are ordinary and inexpensive and fairly conventional. It is the operation of this design rather than its formal resolution, which is exceptional.

Although the word alameda implies that the route should be tree-lined, the emphasis in the design of the new streets seems to be on the hardware rather than on the trees and their establishment. There is no doubt that the establishment of tree-lined boulevards could transform parts of the city. Peñalosa has alluded to the potential of tree planting saying "we could never have Nôtre Dame…[but] imagine a tropical city lined with giant tropical trees…Paris could not have that, it gives us self-esteem."[1] If this approach were taken with the Alameda El Porvenir avenues of trees could provide much-needed shade and shelter, identity and improved amenity for the surrounding neighborhoods and would increase habitat for urban wildlife. The scale of mature tree planting would have a much more significant visual impact on the surroundings than a paved road. The establishment of trees is relatively inexpensive in comparison to the construction of built works, but it does require a steady commitment to ongoing maintenance. Perhaps it is also easier to see the immediate benefits of a constructed object such as the road, with its clear transit function, than the more nebulous future qualitative benefits of avenues of mature trees. In the long term however the benefit of extensive tree planting in terms of character, identity, climatic amelioration and habitat would be considerable.

Unsurprisingly, the project has suffered a certain amount of vandalism and theft since its implementation, and the loss of street lighting has rendered some areas increasingly unsafe at night. Given the social ambitions of the project, and the urban conditions it is trying to improve, this is inevitable and only its ongoing use by the people of the neighborhoods it serves will force its continuing improvement and maintenance. The Alameda El Porvenir resulted from the powerful vision and political commitment of one administration. Urban improvements need the dimension of ongoing maintenance and the supporting infrastructure to continually develop. Its scale and the importance of its continuity mean that this project in particular will require the ongoing support of the city as well as its users to be successful.

HIGHWAY AS CULTURAL LANDSCAPE

Until recently in highway design, the road users' experience has been privileged and the road had been designed as a unified linear element separated from whatever it passes through, and most commonly the landscape has been designed as a special one associated only with the road. The design has traditionally been dominated by highway engineers charged with fulfilling the technical requirements of moving vehicles as fast, efficiently and as safely as possible. It is only more recently that highway design has been more focused on the impact of the road on the landscapes through which it passes, the experience of the driver and passengers of the landscape they move through, and the road landscape as a public landscape and as a functioning ecological system.

The A13 Artscape attempts to change people's experience of driving the road and to influence their understanding of the landscape it passes through by the incorporation of an extensive series of art installations. The art works include landscape works, lighting, sculpture and street furniture.

Even where road design and art interventions are to some extent integrated, as they are in the A13 project, a deeply rooted and persistent conceptual separation tends to limit the role of the art interventions in the design of the total road landscape to something applied. This relates to how the project was conceived rather than how it is being executed. The designers have not used a singular strategy, including a range of works, which perform very different functions within the overall strategy.

Marcel Smets has described different approaches to road design in terms of their relationship to the surrounding landscape He argues for an approach where a new hybrid landscape is created related both to the road and to the landscape through which it passes.[2] This engagement in the A13 Artscape comes about through response to the road's scale and attempts to amplify the experience of the landscape using the technical requirements of the road design and construction and also the cultural landscape.

The relation of speed and scale is the crucial one in road design and needs to be understood visually and experientially as well as technically. The design of road landscapes rarely responds fully to the potential of scale, speed and movement as described by Appleyard et al. "Beyond the concentration on near detail, the fundamental sensation of the road, continuously referred to, is the visual sense of motion and space. This includes the sense of motion of self, the apparent motion of surrounding objects, and the shape of the space being moved through."[3] In this project the various elements respond to the road's scale; a series of towers, a rhythmic avenue of trees (1 mile in length), extensive earthwork forms and hedgerow plantings. Sculptural pieces such as "Holding Pattern" are designed to use the viewer's movement to create a dynamic and changing experience.

Different elements draw from the areas history and cultural landscape, such as hedgerows and tree planting and the use of traditional materials. Others are generated by the technical and engineering requirements of the road: sound barriers, underpasses, fencing, lighting and roundabouts. Many of the works use the materials of the ordinary road landscape to create moments of enhanced or amplified experience: fencing, turf-covered mounds, asphalt, lighting, and tree planting.

DOWNTOWN STREETS AS URBAN SPACES

Macon Yards raises all the issues of town center regeneration projects that have been in play since the 1970s: economic revitalization of depressed downtown areas, reclaiming pedestrian space in the streets, enlivening urban downtowns and enriching them with public art and increased amenity. Initially pedestrian malls and then "main street" approaches were used but Macon Yards is an example of a more complex and sophisticated solution to the problem, drawing from both historical typologies and contemporary ideas.

Selected through a design competition, the project attempts to do all of these things as well as implementing more environmentally appropriate water management techniques for drainage and run-off.

Although by no means radical, there were very few elements of the competition design that were conventional. The design's most significant structural move is that public space has been reclaimed from traffic space, to create a generous central median or *rambla*, which allows a range of new uses to enliven the street. The traffic space is unusual in that it is flexible and is explicitly designed to serve the needs of both drivers and pedestrians. To this end the parking areas are designed to operate as shaded spaces opening to the central "yard" areas, places for people to occupy as well as for car storage. These parking areas are designed with the intention of urban amenity and the acknowledgement of their vital role in the urban experience. The major avenue plantings of the original design also have the potential to transform the character of the space as well as providing much needed shade and shelter. They recall the contribution of street trees in cities like Savannah and New Orleans.

In functional terms the incorporation of other uses with the central yard spaces serves to give them an animation and make them a functioning part of the downtown. The public transit nodes, city market, restrooms would draw people into the space.

The incorporation of remnants of past uses, the preservation and marking of foundations, a wall memorializing famous local musicians and formal reference to historical events and practices all serve to connect the project to the community and its history. The literal quality of these elements as described in the drawings makes them very publicly accessible and attractive. History and memory are usually uncontroversial means to involve communities and give their contributions a tangible form. Most commonly manifest in decorative or formal elements however, while often very popular at the time of a project's completion, it is not these elements that will ensure the project's long term success in becoming a vital and functioning part of the city's life. It is often the structural decisions about space-making and the connections to key urban generators like public transit, which are less easy to explain and less immediately imageable, that drive urban vitality.

Hood's concept of the "yards" and his attempt to create spaces that draw from the character of southern yards and squares is potentially more significant to the experience of Macon's inhabitants. This would change people's behavior in Poplar Street and transform the experience of parking and leaving the car. The removal of the bus station from its integration within the project has unfortunately robbed it of a surefire generator of activity and population.

It appears that as the project moves towards implementation, the forces of regulation, standardization and traffic engineering, and the municipal desire for segregation of uses, are driving it towards a more conventional and generic solution. Some of the most interesting aspects of the project, such as the strong avenue planting and the integration of public transit, are the things that are being whittled away as the project proceeds towards construction. Like so many projects of this type, the design scrutiny and public involvement of the earlier phases fade away over time and decision makers are unprepared to implement an innovative, non-standard solution, despite the fact that this was the basis of the project's initial selection. It is the designer's role to fight on, year after year, to convince everyone involved of the feasibility and desirability of the project, of every design element, fitting and material. Hood's tenacity to date suggests that he will see this project through into implementation, perhaps not in total fulfillment of his original vision, but certainly in a significant urban regeneration through new variations on public space.

[1] Enrique Peñalosa, "Bogotá," presented at the Two Americas Conference, Harvard Design School, February 28–March 1, 2003

[2] Marcel Smets, "The Contemporary Landscape of Europe's Infrastructures" in *Lotus International* (n.110, 2002): 116-125

[3] Donald Appleyard, Kevin Lynch and John R. Myer, *The View from the Road* (Joint Center for Urban Studies of the Massachusetts Institute of Technology and Harvard University; MIT Press, Cambridge Massachusetts, 1964): 8

INFORMATION
IN
PLACE

No one is quite sure how to define a culture of innovation, but they know it when they see it flourish, and individuals, governments, corporations, arts organizations, and universities all want to foster one. In recent years, information technologies have been held up as harbingers of new, networked societies capable of creating unprecedented cultural and economic wealth. This vision's shine may have dulled since 2000, but there is still a deep-seated confidence that the value of information will only rise, and that public space at its best can be a vehicle and vessel for distributing information, whether via old technology, say, a chance discussion in a rain-covered walkway in Asia, or through digital art on the New England coast.

In **Seoul, South Korea,** a subway station, normally a site to rush through, now provides a media center, where travelers can access films and videos not available on-line, and take live interactive courses. In **Singapore,** the planning for a new technopolis is based on a commitment to designing public spaces that stimulate the sort of accidental meetings and rapid, informal sharing of ideas, against a background of recreation and urban pleasures, that characterized many of the places that fueled the software and hardware new technology booms of the 1990s. In **Boston, Massachusetts,** a new art museum will offer the straightforward pleasures of a public space on the waterfront, yet will also incorporate screens for digital information and art. Not only will the content be markedly different from the large screen theaters that pepper the great waterfronts of the world, but the theater form will also be inside out—the screen showing outdoors instead of sealed in a black box. For **Liverpool, United Kingdom,** Fourth Grace is a glittering, thin-legged Gargantua of innovation, which when built will shout that the long-suffering port has left behind its industrialized past, and instead offers a technologically advanced structure containing new programs for meetings, arts, media, and communications. Resisting the reductive notion that the future of information is perpetually digital and kinetic, the building's surface will not be swirling with new media, but rather tell its story, according to the designer, through "hieroglyphics" as compelling as the spiraling relief on Trajan's column in Rome.

FOURTH GRACE

OVERVIEW

Fourth Grace is a radical design for a mixed-use development on the banks of the River Mersey, in Liverpool, historically one of northern England's primary port cities. The design was awarded through a two-stage invited competition in 2000, organized by Liverpool Vision, the city center regeneration company, Liverpool City Council and the joint landowners of the proposed site of the redevelopment, the National Museums and Galleries on Merseyside and the North West Development Agency. Fourth Grace is due to be completed in 2007 in time for the city's 800th birthday celebrations.

Liverpool's waterfront is currently dominated by what are locally known as the "Three Graces": the Liver, the Cunard, and the Port of Liverpool Authority buildings, marble and stone monuments to Liverpool's maritime heritage that were built at the turn of the 19th century. The "Fourth Grace" promises to be a 21st-century icon for Liverpool, fifteen minutes walk from the city center and constructed on the former industrial dockside on Pier Head, a 6-acre site immediately south of the Three Graces and north of Albert Dock and the Kings Waterfront development.

DESIGNERS

The striking design of Fourth Grace is the vision of London-based Alsop Architects, headed by Will Alsop, who are known for their intrepid designs that are brightly colored and boldly engineered and look nothing like their surrounding environment. Peckham Library and Media Center in London for which the firm won Britain's Stirling Prize for Architecture in 2000 is daringly multiple in color as is the blue-painted Regional Government Headquarters in Marseilles. The standout appearances and inventive programming of these buildings have undoubtedly helped make Alsop Architects' projects popular attractions.

DESCRIPTION

The Cloud, the centerpiece of the Fourth Grace development is even more dramatic than previous Alsop designs in color, form and location. Situated on the waterfront on the Hill, it forms a new public space elevated above the new home of the National Museums and Galleries on Merseyside (NMGM). Will Alsop describes the Cloud as "three donuts" sitting on top of one another made from steel and glass, each with a floor space of approximately 50,000 square feet. The spherical building, which appears to teeter on slender steel legs, accommodates community facilities such as workshops and an education center, a hotel and business

center, and on the top floor "The Liverpool Lounge," a bar, restaurant and inside and outside viewing gallery with 360° views of the city. Alsop Architects envision the outdoor viewing platform to be a new "high street" for Liverpool.

The building has been designed as primarily public space, which is emphasized by the interstitial spaces that line the periphery of the structure to form small public seating areas and viewing platforms accessed by a ramp that climbs the edge of the building. These spaces appear where the "donuts" do not sit directly on top of one another and the resultant gaps allow light to penetrate the building and afford views of the city.

One of the most striking elements of the building's design, apart from its memorable shape, is the façade treatment. Wanting to make the entire skin of the building resonate with information about Liverpool, Alsop Architects have designed a ribbon of glass running around the edges that will be etched or screen-printed with contemporary "hieroglyphics." Abstract shapes and symbols tell the story of 800 years of Liverpool, inspired by Trajans Column in Rome, which has a relief that spirals up the column depicting Trajan's two Dacian wars. At night when the building is illuminated, the hieroglyphics will be clearly visible from afar and during the day experienced up close. In an age when high-tech media walls proliferate in architectural designs, Alsop Architects' reinterpretation of a conventional pictorial technique is an innovative information system.

Defined by its multiple public spaces, the approximately $40 million Fourth Grace development also encompasses an infrastructure program that realigns the city with the waterfront. Similar to many post-industrial waterfront cities around the world, Liverpool's waterfront and historic docks are severed from the city center by a six-lane highway. To remedy this, Alsop Architects' scheme includes a bridge over the highway connecting a main artery through the city to the riverfront. There are new water links including a reinstated rail line, a bus/coach/taxi interchange, a new canal, and a 'green' passenger terminal for Mersey Ferries. A series of bridges to the east of the site connects Fourth Grace with the Liverpool Tate gallery, Albert Docks, Maritime Museum and the headquarters of Granada TV.

OUTLOOK

It is hoped that the Fourth Grace will create a signature building that will be of permanent benefit to the city, putting it on the map as the Guggenheim has done in Bilbao and be the linchpin of the projects for 2008, when Liverpool celebrates Cultural Capital of Europe status.

View of Fourth Grace mixed-use development on the River Mersey, Liverpool, United Kingdom. The Cloud, a business and cultural center with a viewing terrace on top, at right. and the Port of Liverpool Authority building, at left

RENDERING: VIRTUAL ARTWORKS (LONDON) 2002

View of Fourth Grace

RENDERING: VIRTUAL ARTWORKS (LONDON) 2002

"The Liverpool Lounge is an elevated public space. It is important to have the possibility to look at the city from a new perspective and to see the place where you live."

WILL ALSOP, ALSOP ARCHITECTS

"This bold choice comes after a stimulating debate in the city. It says a lot for the winner that such a new and original concept should have drawn significant levels of public support in competition with designs which were more traditional and people might feel more comfortable with."

MIKE STOREY,
LEADER OF LIVERPOOL CITY COUNCIL

ONE-NORTH SINGAPORE SCIENCE HUB

SINGAPORE
MASTER PLAN BY ZAHA HADID ARCHITECTS

OVERVIEW

In Spring 2001, Zaha Hadid Architects won an international competition for the planning and initial design phase of a 494-acre district in Singapore, adjacent to the National University, at the intersection of existing and soon to be completed rapid transit lines. The district was conceived of as a "technopole" capable of incorporating and encouraging information-driven industries with the type of active urban environments that would overcome the "new town" sterility familiar from Asia to the Americas. To do this, the physical form and program of the project's public spaces have been designed as the conceptual, visual, and experiential core of the Science Hub's masterplan.

DESIGNER

Zaha Hadid Architects' capacity to design at the boundary of landscape and building, conceiving both small and large projects as urban landscapes, has been evident since the highly influential, though unbuilt "Hong Kong Peak" drawings of 1982. At a time when most urban thinkers were looking backwards, the "Peak" offered up a bedazzling image of luminous geometries promising a renewed modern urbanity. Since that time, the practice, headed by Iraqi-born and London-based Zaha Hadid, has not only won a slew of competitions that called for projects at the boundary of architecture and urban design, but has been completing buildings and master plans around the world, from the Rosenthal Center for Contemporary Art in Cincinnati (open 2003), to the Wolfsburg Science Center in Germany (open 2003). With one-north, Hadid's ability to translate a program's requirements into a sequence of intense and memorable spatial experiences will be brought to bear at the scale of urban planning.

DESCRIPTION

For one-north, the project team has devised a master plan that insists on a strong visual organizing premise, challenging the widespread notion that planning and the way things look bear no relationship. At its center will be two features, the broad, curving Buona Vista Park as the projects's spine, deliberately underprogrammed, and the highly charged Xchanges, which will give separate foci

for the key industries in the technopole: biomedical, and information and communications technology. The visual form offers a coherence and orientation that will be legible to even the casual visitor: the large park at the center, a sculpted profile of buildings rising up like a landscape to either side, and the smaller parks that meld into the "thickened" public space of the Xchanges.

As the project team has pointed out, recent history in Singapore often produced widely separated towers, each in pursuit of an open view, dulling the cityscape, whether from the office or the ground. In addition, the heat, humidity, and rain that typify Singapore's climate through much of the year have hindered the easy give-and-take of indoors and outdoors possible in more temperate climates. One-north offers, by contrast, a "new landscape that aims to achieve Singapore's necessary density without its characteristic patterns of interiorization and segregation," as project consultant Lawrence Barth writes, adding: "This demands an urbanism as attentive to public volumes as to private ones."

The Xchanges are key to this three-dimensional vision, integrated into "networks of calm and introspective locations across the site," even as they offer up "covered walks doubling as showcases, activity zones, and meeting places" extending the "built environment into the park." The parks, paths, and atria are designed to overcome the dull uniformity of "subway-to-office" or "highway-to-parking garage-to-office" planning of the last century.

OUTLOOK

Can a vigorously three-dimensional urban plan actually achieve the visual and programmatic complexity of the "heritage" streets, some of which remain in Singapore and on the one-north site itself? Can a project programmed as a hybrid "campus" and "city" provide a compelling urban experience, bubbling with innovation and opportunity? Will it help Singapore compete in the world marketplace for talent—attracting the young and the skilled from Singapore and beyond who might otherwise head to international high-tech corridors at the other side of the Pacific? One-north offers an ingenious armature for finding out.

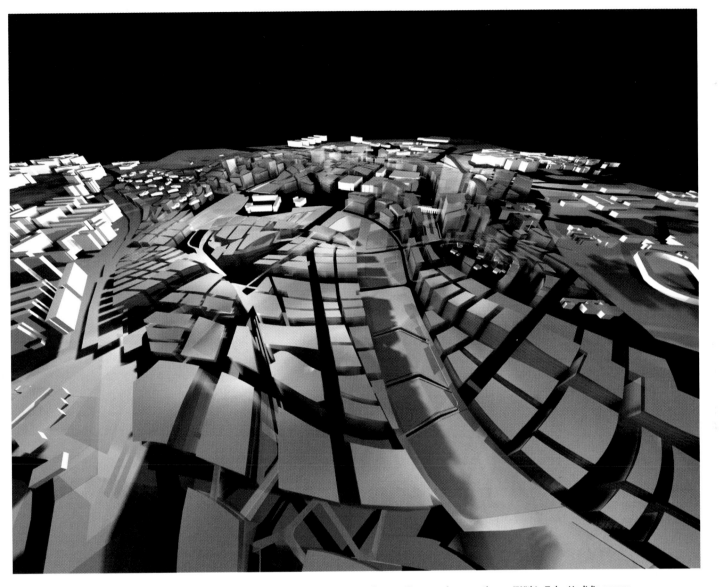

View of One-North Singapore Science Hub

RENDERING: ZAHA HADID ARCHITECTS

"The significance of one-north to the nation's economic and metropolitan strategies can hardly be exaggerated, and for this reason the plan must have a vision reaching well beyond the science parks dotting the world's urban industrial landscape in recent decades. Zaha Hadid's master plan radically departs from the isolation and mono-dimensionality of those developments, acknowledging and incorporating the powerful synergies between urban life and today's research-driven industries."

LAWRENCE BARTH,
URBAN STRATEGY CONSULTANT
TO THE MASTER PLAN

"Within Zaha Hadid's oeuvre there is a long series of urban schemes which explore various artificial landscapes as a means to sculpt public space and to impregnate it with public program. These schemes manipulate and multiply the ground surface by means of sloping, warping, peeling or terracing the ground."

ZAHA HADID ARCHITECTS

INSTITUTE OF CONTEMPORARY ART

BOSTON, MASSACHUSETTS
DILLER + SCOFIDIO

OVERVIEW

What immediately strikes you about Diller + Scofidio's design for the Institute of Contemporary Art in Boston, scheduled to open in 2006, is the attention given to the public spaces around it, which visually and physically extend into the museum. Stepped auditorium seating unfolds from the wooden decking of the HarborWalk, a waterfront promenade that continues to the north and west sides and stretches up to meet the museum's façade. Pedestrians can stroll past the building or come to rest, and enjoy views of the Harbor. The wood of the decking and steps is extended inside the museum, blurring distinctions between inside and outside and enhancing the transparent nature of the museum. This is further augmented by the glazed exterior of the 5,300-square-foot indoor performance space, which can be controlled from full transparency, to partial view, to no view, and total blackout. Films and multi-media projections can be viewed from inside and outside the museum.

DESIGNERS

Elizabeth Diller and Ricardo Scofidio established their studio Diller + Scofidio in 1979 and work on projects that span architecture, the visual arts, and the performing arts. They are recipients of the MacArthur Foundation Award, the first given to architects. In February 2003 they received the commission to redesign Lincoln Center for the Performing Arts' public spaces in association with Fox & Fowle Architects and Cooper Robertson & Partners.

DESCRIPTION

The Boston ICA, which is located on Fan Pier in Boston, overlooking the harbor, is part of a waterfront development being undertaken by the Chicago-based Pritzker family. Aside from the one-acre parcel of land dedicated to the museum, the development will include 107,000-square-feet of civic and cultural space, several acres of parks and open areas, as well as residences, a hotel, and a marina.

The 62,000-square-foot museum will provide triple the space of the ICA's current location with offices, a restaurant and outdoor eating area, a bookstore and a two-story education center with workshops. The main feature of the galleries is their position, cantilevered over the HarborWalk. The overhanging orthogonal 18,000-square-foot gallery ingeniously provides shelter to the public space underneath as well as giving an additional viewing platform above ground. A lenticular glass wall, composed of microscopic vertical lenses, facing the harbor permits vision when viewed from a perpendicular direction and blocks views when viewed from an angle. The 5,300-square-foot indoor performance space has a glazed façade that can be controlled from full transparency, to partial view and no view, to total blackout. Films and multi-media projections can be viewed from inside and outside the museum increasing public participation in the program of the museum. An additional, enclosed stepped-out space with views of the water acts as a digital media center with computer stations where visitors can access digital artworks and the Internet. Illuminated at night, the space becomes a glowing box on the water. A 165-square-foot elevator affords views of the water as visitors ascend or descend the building.

OUTLOOK

A number of major formal moves in the design such as the cantilevered galleries, will need to be fleshed out to allow a structure to be built in the air over the HarborWalk. However, the public spaces that are intrinsic to the building's design and character, which both gallery-goers and users of the HarborWalk can benefit from, will ensure that the ICA is not just an isolated gesture but an integrated component of Boston's waterfront and one that can be enjoyed from the inside and out.

View of the Institute of Contemporary Art, Fan Pier, Boston, Massachusetts, looking southeast

RENDERING: DILLER + SCOFIDIO

"The design of the ICA negotiates between two competing objectives: to perform as a dynamic civic building filled with public and social activities, and as a contemplative space providing individual visitors with intimate experiences with contemporary art."

ELIZABETH DILLER,
DILLER + SCOFIDIO

"We have sought to create…a much loved gathering place for the people of Boston."

VIN COPOLLA,
CHAIRMAN OF THE ICA
BOARD OF TRUSTEES

CHUNGMURO INTERMEDIA PLAYGROUND

CHUNGMURO SUBWAY STATION,
SEOUL, SOUTH KOREA
CHO SLADE ARCHITECTURE WITH TEAM BAHN

OVERVIEW

The Chungmuro Intermedia Playground, a digital media center located in the Chungmuro subway station in the heart of Seoul, was conceived in 2001 as part of a citywide improvement program to upgrade and make use of underutilized public spaces. Since the non-profit center, funded by the city, opened in 2002, it has attracted more than 2,000 members with approximately 50 new members joining weekly. Initiated by the city government, the scheme was prompted by the 2002 World Cup, which was staged in Japan and South Korea, with Seoul being one of the primary host cities.

DESIGNERS/SPONSORS

Cho Slade Architecture, a firm with offices in New York and Seoul, headed by James Slade and Minsuk Cho, in association with Kwang-Soo Kim, principal of team BAHN, an urban research and architecture office based in Seoul, were invited to develop a design for a digital media center within the bowels of Chungmuro subway station. Chungmuro is the center of the city's film industry and near to the offices of the Independent Filmmakers Association who collaborated on the project with the designers in association with the city's transit authority.

DESCRIPTION

Within an existing 1,640-square-foot passageway that connects the entrance of the subway station to the platforms, the designers were charged with creating a media center that was open to the public while at the same time maintaining a thoroughfare for passengers.

The result is a narrow 210-foot-long space enclosed with glass and mirrors with an adjacent five-foot-wide corridor for commuters that runs parallel to the center. Views into both areas visually connect the spaces and encourage passersby to learn more about its facilities.

The linear space incorporates a lounge, video viewing room, study rooms, an editing suite, and exhibition spaces. It is broken up by what Cho Slade refers to as a kaleidoscopic effect created through the use of glass and mirrored walls. Slanted at diagonals, walls generate a row of triangular shaped rooms that run the length of the space. Through movement and reflection Cho Slade explain that, "the experience of depth and amplitude allows both the idea of passage–travel and destination–arrival to exist simultaneously." Altering the angles of the perpendicular space also gave the architects the opportunity to incorporate a multitude of programs within an otherwise confined area.

Visitors enter the center through a glass lobby, which leads into a lounge with magazines and TVs for viewing videos that can be borrowed from the video and digital media art library located behind with the offices, which specializes in hard-to-find art films. Two classrooms and a small viewing room with three screens follow and next to these is a larger screening room with stepped seating. Each room employs a bold use of color, predominantly black and red. In the main screening gallery, a curtain wall made from silver chain embedded between two sheets of tinted glass can be pulled across the glass window to provide a more controlled environment when needed and prevent light entering the room so artworks can be viewed. The back wall of this space can be opened to connect it with the contiguous gallery space, which presents work by emerging Korean media artists and students.

OUTLOOK

The Chungmuro Intermedia Playground is free to join. A nominal fee of approximately $1 is charged to view videos, and a two-week digital editing course costs $50. The media center introduces a new type of facility into the subway and animates the subway passages as public spaces that can provide activities other than catching a train.

① 동국대학교후문입구
To Dongguk Univ. Back Gate
② 필동사무소 ⑨ 중구청
Pil-dong Office   Jung-gu Office

View of video screening auditorium of Chungmuro Internedia Playground.

PHOTO: JUNG-SIK MOON

View of the entrance to the Intermedia Playground, a film and digital media center in Chungmuro Subway Station, Seoul, South Korea

PHOTO: JUNG-SIK MOON

"Mass transit is no longer just a line connecting two functions: technology allows the extension of these functions into the line transforming it into a new entity."

JAMES SLADE,
CHO SLADE ARCHITECTURE

"The idea was to create an interactive environment that was as inclusive as possible. Open from 11am to 8pm everyday it is a place that can be used by anyone from a commuter to a film student."

MINSUK CHO,
CHO SLADE ARCHITECTURE

"Seoul City and Korail operate more than 250 subway stations, most of them pretty much alike. A few, however, linger in the memory. At Chungmuro Station, where lines 3 and 4 intersect, is a multimedia oasis for culture-thirsty train riders."

YOON JA-YOUNG, *THE KOREA TIMES*

WILL ALSOP SPEAKS OUT

The following transcript is from a telephone conversation between architect **Will Alsop** and **Zoë Ryan,** *OPEN* Exhibition Curator that took place in September 2003. Will Alsop, director of Alsop Architects in London recently designed the Fourth Grace (featured in the *OPEN* exhibit), the winning scheme for a new waterfront development in Liverpool, centered around a cultural and business facility, to be completed in 2008 to coincide with Liverpool's festivities as European Capital of Culture

ZOË RYAN: Could you explain your approach to working with the public on large-scale projects?

WILL ALSOP: What interests me about large-scale projects is that I know before I start that whatever I design will not be done. Well what's the point then? The point is that hopefully the overall plan that I have developed will change the current situation, create aspirations and lift the city. Eventually I might get the opportunity to design one of the buildings within the plan, which then becomes a model for the project's goals and creates expectations of what could happen if the entire scheme were realized. For example, for a project I am working on in Barnsley in the UK as part of the projects being undertaken by Yorkshire Forward's Urban Renaissance Panel—is foremost a process of discovering what this city might like to be. Working with local people, politicians, business people, etc., I deliberately try to go beyond what I know and learn from that.

There are lots of models for public design processes that haven't worked such as Potsdamer Platz in Berlin. There were endless discussions but what actually came out of them was very disappointing as shown in the architecture of the site. There was also nothing on paper to reveal those discussions and to point to during or after the process.

However, for projects in which I have been more heavily involved with the public I have organized workshops that try and get the public to imagine their city in 10 years and describe the place and the things they might be doing. I have a method that I employ for the workshops. First, I ask each person to write down their thoughts and then read them out to each other in order to break down the barriers between them. The process can be difficult at first, but given the right atmosphere and perseverance by the end of the discussion people are adding to their comments and changing their descriptions and there is a buzz around the project. I am interested in building aspirations and going beyond the dull desires of "We want bigger roads, and more parking and houses." We very often film this process so we have a record and can refer to it at a later stage.

Next, I ask the workshop participants to illustrate their ideas. Everyone immediately says they can't draw, which is a shame. In the late Victorian era everyone could draw, or was not afraid to express themselves through drawing. However, after a while people relax and begin to visualize their ideas on paper.

The drawings and comments are important signifiers and illustrations of the process, which I take away to study and from which I draw inspiration. My designs become an interpretation of this public feedback. These materials are useful to show when explaining the final design so people understand your point of departure. In addition, we often present the films we made during the workshops in the local cinema. Often the only people who read the reports on the design process are the press and they look for contentious issues with which to make a good story. The film is an accessible way for the general public to see how the design process was managed and understand the context and scope of the project. Local press, politicians, and the public can watch it together and this approach normally staves of any negative reports from the press and can be an effective way of gaining support. The presentation of the film and the materials from the workshops can be crucial in getting the public to accept more radical ideas. If I simply propose a project, without public input and without showing them the diversity of ideas and the amount of public interaction that took place at the workshops, the public is often hostile.

RYAN: Broadcasting is an important aspect of your practice. Do you have filmmakers on staff?

ALSOP: We have four. At the moment I am interested in developing ideas for a local television channel, which discusses issues such as architecture and urban planning; a virtual public space that the public could contribute to. For example, the district plan that I am working on in Barnsley will require that any future planning documents are in accordance with this plan. It is a very rigid way of working and does not leave much room for flexibility. Who can tell if the plan will be relevant in 10-15 years time? It may require rapid adjustment but at present there are no mechanisms in place to allow that to happen. A television program that could explain this would be a very intelligent way to provide a public forum for these types of issues.

RYAN: You recently completed three television programs for Channel 4 called "Super Cities." How did this project come about?

ALSOP: Channel 4 asked me to propose a series of programs looking at some of the ideas I had been developing in my work. Inspired by my work in the north of England I came up with the "Super Cities" concept. For example, the first program, "Coast to Coast" looks at the area from Hull to Liverpool, which has a population of 15.4 million people, who are connected by the M62 motorway. More and more, people are traveling from one city to another to get the things they want. For example, if you are in Manchester and want a good curry you can go to Bradford, and from there, to Hull, if you want a good market. This is what I call a "Super City": urban developments that stretch along communication routes and extend between cities. These areas are becoming more urbanized in character and require new identities. Of course, we hope the Fourth Grace will attract people to Liverpool. The second program, called "Diagonal," looks at the area from Birmingham in the center of England, to London and finally Southend Pier, on the Essex coast, and the third program "Waves," stretches along the south coast from Hastings, in Sussex, to Poole, in Dorset.

My architecture practice is interested in attracting people to city centers like Liverpool, as with Fourth Grace, however, in the next 5-10 years the UK will be faced with other concerns. One of these is that thousands of new homes will be needed and along with that comes an increase in transportation; an increasing reliance on the car and the services that are needed to support car culture. I am interested in looking into what I call "hot spots," new villages along these green belts between cities that have a density that can sustain high-rise residences accommodating 3-4,000 people in one building, taking advantage of the landscape and views. This is one of the ideas I discuss in the program.

RYAN: Your work for the Fourth Grace has involved envisioning a program and concept for this area of Liverpool as well as leading architecture and design considerations. What does it take to pull one of these projects together in terms of monetary support, political resources, interest in design, etc?

ALSOP: The Fourth Grace is different as it was a competition, but a public process still exists and I constantly have to prove the value of the experiences that the project will generate to politicians and nearby institutions. My interest, and that of my practice is in good design as a champion of renewal, as well as its best product, but of course we have to get involved in politics and funding sources to some extent. My experience is that the more we get involved, the better, as it offers a share in control of the process. Being on the receiving end has been the bugbear of the architectural profession since its inception.

When we first set out thinking about a design, we are conscious of how we can deliver this financially. As this was a developer/architect-led project we were part of a consortium that included Countryside Properties PLC, IDC Ltd, and Neptune Developments Ltd. The idea for the separate high-rise residential tower to be built behind the Fourth Grace was essentially a way to generate income for the project and enable 60% of the Fourth Grace to be kept open for public use. The public spaces are accessible 24 hours a day and by placing the "Liverpool Lounge," a public restaurant, bar, exhibition space, and viewing gallery at the top we have ensured that the building is activated throughout with human presence.

RYAN: How do you envision Fourth Grace providing a legacy after the yearlong events of the 2008 Cultural Capital festival are over and contributing to the longer-term goals of the urban regeneration of Liverpool?

ALSOP: We hope that the building will communicate a great experience and say something about Liverpool at the turn of the century. I don't want it to talk to people in any particular or forced way but show an early 21st century confidence in Liverpool through the quality and function of the building. Cedric Price said that architecture should only be built to last as long as it is required. I think that we should build architecture to last a long time and insure that through the design it will be able to adapt to other functions and uses.

The area around the Fourth Grace is characterized by small-scale operations: galleries and narrow roads. By adding a different dimension in the form of a larger attraction we hope to add contemporary architecture to Liverpool's skyline that people will want to travel to see. While we were making "Super Cities" I went to Coventry Cathedral. Like the Fourth Grace, it was a talking point when it was built. People were surprised by the high quality of the architecture and its magnificent scale. It was a radical building. The Fourth Grace will give a different type of urban grain to Liverpool. We know about the cities of the past, what I am interested in is finding out what we don't know, and changing perceptions and the way we use architecture. When architects do good buildings they receive attention and then they meld into the normality of everyday life but people are always interested in them. That is my hope for the Fourth Grace.

None of the functions of the Fourth Grace are confined to the Year of Culture, although it will play its part in the celebration. I see it as an anchor for the celebrations, having established its own and unique character at the heart of Liverpool in advance of the year's commencement. The museum, hotel, apartments, retail and commercial space will all have their own longevity and momentum, acting as a catalyst for development along the entire waterfront.

RYAN: In the *OPEN* exhibit Fourth Grace features within the theme of "Information." Information and community is key to your process but we are also interested in how you see information in cities evolving. In today's cities, information is often oversimplified as just public adverts in the subway and new technologies in public space. How do you see Fourth Grace contributing to this dialogue?

ALSOP: The original inspiration for the building was based on a venture from a year earlier called the "City Centre" which was going to be a digital media center for Liverpool, inculcating an awareness of, and access to, digital means of communication for the citizens of Liverpool who may not have access to these. Several elements of this scheme have been transferred to the Fourth Grace and assimilated into the brief, with exemplars of digital communication incorporated into the public and museum areas—which fits with the main premise of the project, which is education, as the ultimate catalyst for renewal and development.

RYAN: Do you ever return to your buildings once they have opened? Have you been back to Peckham Library, for example, to see how it is working?

ALSOP: I often go back. The impetus to return and evaluate a project is the ability to prompt an evolution in the work of the practice so that our responses to the brief keep getting better. Architects have everything to learn from experience, which, to their detriment, has too much been neglected in the past in favor of theory or dogma—a stance that I repudiate. My work is an endless exploration in improving and investigating experiences through architecture. However, I'm not into finding a recipe for a successful project. Life is not like that.

NEW MEETING GROUNDS

People assemble, by the dozens to the millions, for reasons ranging from religion to rock, to enact everything from ancient rituals to rites of passage invented last week. Whether in the center of the city or its edge, these are usually held in an urban context, and there is often a struggle to take a well-known type of program—a fairground in Latin America, an art space in Asia, a performance arts park in Europe, and give it new relevance by its form and site.

In **Graz, Austria,** an artist designed a performance hall for a temporary island in the middle of the river, the focus of a large arts and events program for the city. In **Tokyo, Japan,** a new district declares itself a new landscape, calling itself the "hills" where there have been none. The buildings are the hills, covered in greenery and gardens, and at the core is a new art gallery, at the top of a colossal high-rise, occupying the building almost as though the tower were a landscape, or a horizontal extension of the city rotated to the vertical. Instead of being sited on a plaza like many museums, the gallery is adjacent to a "street in the sky," achieving what many still considered farfetched in some recent proposals for the World Trade Center site and other dense urban areas. At the edge of **Guadalajara, Mexico,** a new district, to date still a virtual showcase of design talent, but expected to break ground soon, includes a vast area that will master its scale through design elements that will define its multiple roles as a market and exhibition site. **Barcelona, Spain** has been an international leader in creating new and revived public spaces as part of massive capital construction campaigns, linked conceptually and financially to programs such as the Olympics, and most recently, the Universal Forum of Cultures scheduled for 2004. A new waterfront park in the Catalonian capital will be a new landscape, its rising and falling waves of ground in stark contrast to an earlier generation of the city's projects, demonstrating its perpetual search for new forms and new programs. In **Amsterdam, the Netherlands,** a former gas-works whose buildings have already been occupied by activities from art studios to rave parties, has been organized into a new landscape that accommodates the local neighborhood's demand for green space and the Dutch passion for korfball, together with the larger district's emerging demand for arts programming. The design, which had to address severe contaminants on the site, embodies the past three hundred years of the West's attitudes towards the use and abuse of urban land.

WESTERGASFABRIEK PARK

AMSTERDAM, THE NETHERLANDS
GUSTAFSON PORTER, LTD.

OVERVIEW

Opened in September 2003, the Westergasfabriek Park provides Amsterdam with a major recreational and cultural destination. Situated to the west of the city center between the railway line to Haarlem and the district of Staatsliedenbuurt, the park retains 22 of the buildings of the municipal power company's former gasworks, including one of the former gas tanks. After the plant closed in the 1960s, the site and buildings were used for storage and parking until 1992, when they came into the ownership of the Westerpark City District Council. With the support of the local advocacy group Friends of Westerpark, the Council put out a call for ideas and received over 300 responses. As a consequence, the Council conducted tests on the contaminated soil to determine what was necessary to transform this brownfield site into a usable park, and established an events office to rent out the buildings on a temporary basis.

DESIGNER

In 1997, the Council organized an invited international design competition for the park, won by American landscape architect Kathryn Gustafson, whose London partnership Gustafson Porter with Neil Porter worked on the design. For Gustafson, meeting the Amsterdam Park's functional requirements was also an opportunity to take an intellectual stance on changing attitudes to landscape. The industrial gasworks site has an existing public park, Westerpark, laid out as an "English Garden" on its east side. The design responds to that and to the industrial brownfield by creating a succession of uses and experiences in space from east to west. These represent a progression of attitudes towards landscape, from identifying the site as primarily for programmed functions, to a "pure" nature/ecology approach in the polders to the northwest, and finally reaching a sculpture park at the western tip. Together they embody a contemporary attitude, which reintegrates humans into an ecologically based understanding of the land.

DESCRIPTION

At the southeast corner, the market place forms the main entrance to the park. Steel is a predominant material here in a series of lighting posts and bands inlaid into the paving as directional markers between the buildings which will house theaters, restaurants, design studios and galleries.

At the east entrance is a field of hedgerows and rose bushes. North Plaza, planted with Elm and European Beech trees borders the events field. The 18,000 square foot lake that culminates at the North Plaza is bordered by black limestone that peaks at the outermost edges to form benches overlooking the water. The water in the lake is recycled as it drains through a weir at its east end. Wind and water sculptures are positioned throughout the lake and a fountain at the northeast edge acts as a visual feature as well as a natural sound barrier against passing trains. A grass-covered amphitheatre is at the edge of the events field.

Running diagonally across the park is the main axis, Broadway, that ends at the former site of two gas tanks at the southwest corner and sculpture park. At its eastern edge, a forest of Rhododendrons and Azaleas creates "sheltered" rooms for reading or relaxing.

North of this area is the remaining gas tank, transformed by the Dutch architecture firm Mecanoo into a theater space. Behind this is a korfball field and two smaller buildings for children's indoor activities.

OUTLOOK

Westergasfabriek Park provides Amsterdam with both intimate and large-scale public spaces for a range of recreational and cultural activities that have already played host to the Holland Festival and the Drum Rhythm Festival, among others, and manages to both meet the immediate neighborhood's desire for open space and sports with broader needs for space for cultural events.

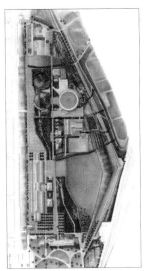

Plan of Westergasfabriek Park,
Amsterdam, the Netherlands

DRAWING: GUSTAFSON PORTER, LTD/
MECANOO ARCHITECTS

Aerial view of Westergasfabriek
Park

PHOTO: PROJECTBUREAU
WESTERGASFABRIEK

Aerial view of Westergasfabriek Park, Amsterdam, the Netherlands,
showing existing Wester Park in foreground and polders in background

PHOTO: PROJECTBUREAU WESTERGASFABRIEK

"Today we interpret the use of public space in a new way and are able to focus on places that had different value twenty years ago. This will continue as we explore how to repair and rescue damaged lands in our industrialized society. In this evolution, a bold intellectual stance and rich emotional palette are essential to creating landscapes that carry a sense of function, time and place. "

KATHRYN GUSTAFSON, IN JANE AMIDON, *RADICAL LANDSCAPES* (THAMES & HUDSON)

"It is very important that people see the park as their public space...where buildings and the environment complement each other and where something will be happening 24 hours a day."

EVERT VERHAGEN,
PROJECT DIRECTOR,
WESTERGASFABRIEK, AMSTERDAM

JVC CULTURE, CONVENTION AND BUSINESS CENTER

GUADALAJARA, MEXICO
CARME PINÓS STUDIO

OVERVIEW

Construction of the JVC Culture, Convention and Business Center is scheduled to begin in 2005 on the northeastern edge of the city of Guadalajara, capital of the state of Jalisco, in Mexico. The project will span across 600 acres, and will bring Guadalajara, a city with a population of approximately five million, a much needed cultural and business center. The development, spearheaded by Jorge Vergara, CEO of Omnilife, and named in honor of his father Jorge Vergara Cabrera, is a $500-million project, which includes a convention center, offices, an entertainment and shopping complex, museums, a hotel, an amphitheater, a university, and even a palenque—a traditional cockfighting ring. More than half the site will be given over to public space including a 96-acre park with a fairground and market place designed by Spanish architect Carme Pinós. It will be the anchor-site of the annual Feast of October festival that attracts millions of visitors.

DESIGNER

Based in Barcelona, Carme Pinós established her own office, Carme Pinós Studio, in 1991 after ending a decade-long partnership with architect Enric Miralles. Together they became well known for such award-winning projects as the Igualada Cemetry in Spain and a building for an archery range for the 1992 Olympic Games. For her own work, Carme Pinós was awarded the Spanish National Architecture Prize in 1995 for the Morella boarding school and the Valencia Government's Institute of Architects Prize in 2001 for the Juan Aparicio waterfront in Torrevieja, Spain.

DESCRIPTION

In the late 1990s Mexican architect Enrique Norten of TEN Arquitectos was invited by Vergara to select a team of architects to work collectively on a master plan for the site. Bordered on the west by La Primavera, a heavily wooded federal reserve, the development will connect to the freeway to the east and the Vallarta Avenue on the northern edge, which runs through Guadalajara. The architects who have worked on the project to date include Wolf Prix, Thom Mayne, Jean Nouvel, Zaha Hadid, Toyo Ito, González de León, Philip Johnson and Alan Ritchie, Daniel Libeskind, and Carme Pinós.

Experienced in designing public spaces around the world, Carme Pinós was charged with creating a fairground that could accommodate a range of programs from art, culture and commerce such as traditional amusement park rides, stalls to service a market place selling food and local crafts and exhibition stands.

The site is currently a cornfield, severed from the rest of the development by a peripheral highway. Pinós' design proposes three buildings that ramp over the road to a plaza adjacent to the convention center by Norten and a shopping and entertainment center by Coop Himmelb(l)au. Visitors can enter the site through the buildings, which will be for rent for exhibitions and other events, as well as via exterior ramps that run alongside the structures. The sculptural bridge-buildings will hang on tension cables from arched frames. The façades will be glass to allow natural ventilation, maximum transparency, and views across the fairgrounds. Not only do the bridge-buildings create a safe passage over the highway but they also allow for the entrance to the site to be programmed. Entrance will be free but the various attractions inside the park will have a fee.

Throughout the roughly semi-circular grounds, stalls made from free-standing, undulating precast concrete canopies supported by central pillars will accommodate a multiplicity of cafés and bars and stands for selling wares and food goods. This "promenade of ribbons" as described by Pinós, creates a rolling landscape on a predominantly flat site that encourages fluid movement. Given the seasonal quality of the festivals and events that have been planned for the site, the stalls have been created so they can be used as shelters to stand and sit under.

OUTLOOK

The JVC Culture, Convention and Business Center is based on the theory that culture will attract business and that in turn business will pay for culture. The project initiates a new concept for Latin American cities that will be infused with local as well as international influences. Carme Pinós' design, on a challenging site set apart from the rest of the development, attempts to make the transition from culture to commerce as seamless as possible by creating a landscape that can be understood as a fairground, market place or outdoor business center and at other times be enjoyed as a park.

View of model of the fairgrounds and bridge-buildings, JVC Culture, Convention and Business Center, Guadalajara, Mexico

PHOTO: CARME PINÓS STUDIO

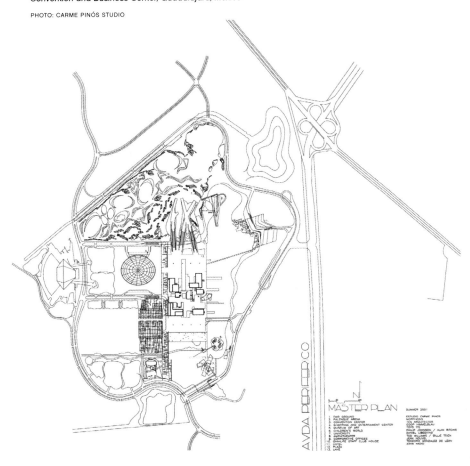

View of master plan of JVC Culture, Convention, and Business Center, Guadalajara, Mexico, showing fairgrounds and bridge-buildings at top of site

DRAWING: CARME PINÓS STUDIO

"A fairground is not a static but a dynamic place. I wanted to create a promenade of ribbons; roofs made from concrete that cover the stands. These sensual elements encourage movement and activity. When they are empty their form gives a rhythm to the park."

CARME PINÓS,
CARME PINÓS STUDIO

MORI ART MUSEUM

ROPPONGI HILLS, TOKYO, JAPAN
GLUCKMAN MAYNER ARCHITECTS AND
KOHN PEDERSEN FOX ASSOCIATES

OVERVIEW

The Mori Art Museum (MAM) designed by New York based architect Richard Gluckman is located on the top two floors of the 53-story Roppongi Tower (designed by Kohn Pedersen Fox) one of a number of buildings that make up the 29-acre Roppongi Hills mixed-use development in central Tokyo. The brainchild of Minoru Mori, the president of Mori Building Company, Roppongi Hills introduces a dense landscape of structures topped with green roofs to a city with a flat topography. From every angle, whether inside or outside the buildings, parks and green spaces are visible.

The 100,000 square-foot Mori Art Museum, dedicated to showing contemporary art is the cynosure of the development. The museum, which spans the top two floors, is housed within the Mori Art Center, with an auditorium, conference rooms, a club designed by British-based Conran & Partners and an educational facility open 24 hours a day, designed by Mori Building Company.

Positioned at the top of Tokyo's tallest office tower, Mori Art Museum is a novel urban space. A 18,500-square-foot viewing terrace that runs around the periphery of the 52nd floor, the "Tokyo City View," also designed by Gluckman Mayner Architects becomes an enclosed "street" above ground. Benches run the length of the space and two cafés serve light refreshments creating a picnic area in the sky. A rooftop viewing platform, "Tokyo Sky Deck" gives unobstructed, 360° views of the city.

DESCRIPTION

Known for their designs for art venues that include the Andy Warhol Museum in Pittsburgh, Gluckman Mayner Architects' primary concern was how the museum is distinguished within the tower. The Museum Cone, an almost 100-foot-tall elliptical glass pavilion acts as the entrance to the museum. Visitors can either ascend the pavilion on foot via a ramp that circles around the interior or can take the elevators located at the center. The lightweight steel and glass façade, engineered by Yoshinori Nito & Dewhurst Macfarlane and Partners is made from steel and fritted glass panels held in place by a diagonal net of ¾-inch tension cables connected to a horizontal ¾-inch steel ring. At the top a short glass walkway takes visitors into Roppongi Tower where they buy tickets for the observation deck and/or the museum. High-speed elevators ascend to the 52nd and 53rd floor.

A shift of 45 degrees along the major axis, physically and visually demarcates the position of the two floors from the rest of the building. Clear orientation is achieved by uninterrupted views through the entire floors and a strong color palette such as the rose back-painted glass entries and exits. Suspended within the four-story, rough, red sandstone Central Atrium, a floating two-story, translucent chartreuse glass elliptical volume orients the visitor, who can travel by escalator between the 50th and 53rd floors.

The main galleries on the 53rd floor are designed to accommodate rotating exhibitions of contemporary art, architecture, film, photography, design, fashion, and media art. The simple, orthogonal galleries run the circumference of the central atrium, divided by movable walls. A lighting system at the top and sides of the elongated galleries creates a bias in the space and encourages movement.

OUTLOOK

Since Le Corbusier first wrote about the "vertical city" in 1931, architects have increasingly striven to push the limits, with all facets of life from business to pleasure located high above ground: a "city within a city." The Mori Art Museum and viewing terraces, open daily until 11pm, activate the tower long after the offices have closed and provide Tokyo with a major contemporary art institution, a unique destination and spectacular lookout point.

View of Mori Art Museum's "Tokyo City View"

PHOTO: GLUCKMAN MAYNER ARCHITECTS

View of the Museum Cone, Mori Art Museum, Roppongi Hills, Tokyo, Japan

PHOTO: GLUCKMAN MAYNER ARCHITECTS

View of Mori Art Museum

PHOTO: GLUCKMAN MAYNER ARCHITECTS

"The Mori Art Museum creates an opportunity for a platform in the sky overlooking Tokyo. It is an iconic crown to an immensely complex urban development."

PAUL KATZ, PARTNER,
KOHN PEDERSEN FOX ASSOCIATES

"The design of the Mori Art Museum interrupts the museological path of conventional exhibition spaces. I wanted to encourage movement through lighting and color so that the galleries aren't static spaces but can accommodate a constantly changing exhibition schedule. At the same time I wanted people to explore the perimeter of the building and look out."

RICHARD GLUCKMAN,
GLUCKMAN MAYNER ARCHITECTS

SOUTH-EAST COASTAL PARK AND AUDITORIUMS

BARCELONA, SPAIN
FOREIGN OFFICE ARCHITECTS

OVERVIEW

In 1999, London-based Foreign Office Architects (FOA) won an international competition to design the South-East Coastal Park and Auditoriums, a project measuring 164,000 square feet with a budget of approximately $12 million. The park, part of the infrastructure for the Universal Forum of Cultures event in 2004 being held in the city has been built on a section of reclaimed land bordered by a major highway, a new waste water treatment plant on the city side and a new bathing area at the seafront. A major venue for concerts and theater performances, the park has two open-air auditoriums, one of which accommodates 10,000 people and another for approximately 5,000 people.

DESIGNERS

Foreign Office Architects, headed by Farshid Moussavi and Alejandro Zaera-Polo, are well known for their designs which subvert the norm of linear architectural forms. Their largest project to date is the Yokohama International Port Terminal in Japan for which they transformed an orthogonal pier into both an undulating surface and a multi-programmed space between the city and the water.

DESCRIPTION

Fundamental to their approach to the park was again a desire to transform the ground into an active surface as well as provide a bridge between the city and the waterfront. The topography they designed for the park is characterized by dunes, which although traditional in beachscapes, are here integrated into a contemporary synthetic landscape.

The physical form of the park was not only prompted by wanting to create a visually interesting landscape, but by more pragmatic concerns. The first is that the site needs to form a connection between the 12-meter high public access platform that ramps over the water treatment plant from the highway and the lower level of the bathing area at the waterfront. The rolling landscape creates an interface between the varying ground levels. The second condition is the abrasive salt breezes from the sea that make it difficult to retain vegetation on the site. With this in mind, FOA have generated a mediated landscape made from precast concrete tiles and sand, in parts planted with reeds, grass and trees that can withstand severe weather conditions. The precast concrete was explicitly selected for its ability to adjust to the settling of the reclaimed land. Zaera-Polo explains that the half-moon shaped tiles are reminiscent of traditional Catalonian mosaics but are here at the scale of an architectural element.

Through extensive topographical research, FOA found that by exploiting the figurative qualities of the landscape, the dunes provide slopes in which to locate bleachers for spectators and in addition give shelter from the weather. These seating areas are located at intervals across the park. Their density increases at the two areas in which they are used as auditoriums.

OUTLOOK

Held from May 9 to September 26, 2004, the Universal Forum of Cultures, an ambitious international event will include exhibitions, conferences, and seminars engaging the topics of sustainable development, cultural diversity and peace. The Forum is an initiative of the Barcelona City Council with the Catalonian and Spanish governments and UNESCO and will be situated in Besòs, a 480-hectare area in the northeastern corner of the city bordered by the sea, the River Besòs and the Barcelona and Sant Adrià municipalities.

The forum is driving urban regeneration on a scale similar to that for the 1992 Olympics in Barcelona. As well as the cultural aspect of the South-East Coastal Park and Auditoriums, by creating an extreme artificial topography FOA hopes to encourage participation and appropriation by a variety of sports and leisure activities. The traceable contour lines of the landscape ensure that a variety of activities from walking and running to biking and skateboarding occur as well as more extreme sports.

Aerial view of the Besòs area of Barcelona, Spain, in the northeastern corner of the city, showing the future site of the South-East Coastal Park and Auditoriums, part of the infrastructure for the Universal Forum of Cultures in 2004

PHOTO: FOREIGN OFFICE ARCHITECTS

Study of topography for the South-East Coastal Park and Auditoriums, Barcelona, Spain

RENDERING: FOREIGN OFFICE ARCHITECTS

"Our design constitutes an alternative to both the rational geometry, artificial, linear, and consistent, and contradictory geometry that intends to reproduce the picturesque qualities of nature."

FOREIGN OFFICE ARCHITECTS

ISLAND IN THE MUR

OVERVIEW

Events such as World Expositions, the Venice art and architecture biennials, the Cultural Capital of Europe program and the Olympics often provide cities with the impetus and the funding to generate a range of new public projects, from buildings to parks and plazas, as well as new facilities such as improved transportation systems. In addition to these large-scale, permanent projects, smaller scale interventions, predominantly organized as temporary events and installations, can be equally important activators encouraging participation and engagement in the city.

DESIGNERS

Island in the Mur, commissioned by Graz 2003, Cultural Capital of Europe was designed by artist Vito Acconci whose office Studio Acconci is based in Brooklyn. Acconci is known for his public works, such as "Flying Floors for Ticketing Pavilion," a series of sculptural resting areas he designed in 1998 for Terminal B/C at Philadelphia International Airport. Asked to create an open-air cultural facility to float on the Mur River in the heart of Graz in Austria, Acconci designed a sculptural steel pod that is connected by two gently curving ramps to the riverbanks. The island idea was conceived of by Robert Punkenhofer, a Graz-based curator and head of the firm Art&Idea, as a way to incorporate the river in the year-long festival and connect the two sides of the city which are bisected by this 275 mile-long international channel of water that runs through Austria, Slovenia, Croatia and Hungary.

DESCRIPTION

The Island in the Mur is one of the focal points of Graz 2003, commissioned for the year-long celebration of art and culture. The 1,500 square foot Island that was three years in the making incorporates an open-air theater with 300 seats for performances, the "Vito" café run by

Graz's traditional bakery and coffee house, Sorger, and a children's playground. Rather than simply placing an orthogonal platform on the water as is more customary, Acconci Studio devised an elegant, fluid form constructed from a latticework of 320 tons of steel and glass. Its sensual form, two shell-like structures, one closed and one open, creating the various spaces, was not only generated by the programmatic needs but by environmental pragmatic requirements. The boat-like structure was designed to allow for the flow of the river and to withstand possible floods. Acconci describes the concept: "One space twists and turns and warps to become the other. A dome twists and turns upside down to become a bowl, while the bowl twists and turns upside down to become a dome." The amphitheater is located in the bowl and the café is situated within the enclosed dome. Where the two forms intersect is the children's playground, a landscape that at points rises and envelopes the roof of the café. "The functions are mixed," explains Acconci. "There's no hierarchy, no boundaries, no separation between inside and outside; the user decides for himself/herself where to set the limits. The playground forms the background to the stage; while you're watching a performance on the stage, there are screaming children in the background, while you're having a drink in the café the children are playing overhead." As well as a performance venue the Island acts as a viewing platform over the city. From deep within the artificial island, views of the city's hilly landscape are still visible through glass windows and slits in the woven steel structure.

OUTLOOK

Generated as a project constructed for a year only, the Island proved so popular with locals and international visitors alike that it was proposed as a permanent structure and remains in the city.

*View of Island in the Mur, Graz, Austria, an outdoor theater,
café and children's playground, part of Graz 2003, European Capital of
Culture*

PHOTO: ELVIRA KLAMMINGER

*Aerial view of Island in the Mur,
Graz, Austria*

PHOTO: HUFTON & CROW © VIEW PICTURES

"We initially wanted to design an island under water—a bubble of air—almost like a fishbowl of air in the middle of the water—but when we found out that the river was not twelve-feet deep but one-foot deep we had to change our plans. We couldn't ground our island; it has to float like a boat."

VITO ACCONCI, ACCONCI STUDIO

"Acconci has 'placed' Island in the Mur directly into the minds of the inhabitants of Graz; they are now suddenly able to appreciate the river again."

WOLFGANG LORENZ,
INTENDANT OF GRAZ 2003-CULTURAL
CAPITAL OF EUROPE

"My vision was to establish a piazza for the new millennium in the center of Graz, in the middle of the water. A platform for communication, contemplation and artistic creation—reconnecting the city with the water, bridging the divided city parts and bringing together people and cultures."

ROBERT PUNKENHOFER, ART&IDEA

PARADOXICAL SPACES

Linda Pollak is Principal of Marpillero Pollak Architects, and Assistant Professor of Architecture, Harvard Design School

The power of paradox…[is] in showing that sense always follows two directions at the same time.[1]

This text establishes a framework in which to consider the evolving role and definition of program in the design of urban spaces. A basic premise, which references shifts in thinking about nature as well as cities, is that a heightening of value of historically recessive or repressed aspects of urban space, such as everyday space, landscape, and transience, is shifting them to a status of program. An interpretation of the five New Meeting Grounds (NMG) projects focuses on how attention, for aspects that might have previously been considered as background in an urban environment, can provide a springboard to explore their potential in new spaces. The text concludes by focusing on how this shift might affect issues of representation.

Each project's approach to program is linked to the way in which it invests in the ground. Whether it is a glowing platform atop a tower conceived as a landform, an island theater, or a topography of concrete, the ground of each project is an active surface in two senses–not only a surface that supports activities, but also a performative element. A performative conception of identity has to do with an understanding of identity as continually being produced. Rather than the meaning of a space existing in an *a priori*, "black and white" sense, it is developed performatively, that is, happening, in the way it is in the world, becoming, a process. This process can be seen as one of negotiation between the terms which constitute it, such that a ground conceived in terms of architecture and landscape would perform as urban space through the interplay between these and other terms.

A positive focus on program does not entail that "form follows function." Public spaces often have little specific use program, or to the extent that this program exists, it may not be the engine of the space. Each of the NMG projects operates not only in terms of the specific program for which the design has been commissioned, but also in terms of what could be called an urban program. As Vito Acconci says about the Island in the Mur: "people go here …to have fun and feel well." This urban program exceeds function. Whether inside or outside, one way to conceptualize it is as everyday space, that is, the non-monumental aspects of urban life. This urban program operates as a social condenser to allow and support interaction.

A critical aspect of programming urban space is the designer's inability to control the outcome. The philosopher Henri Lefevbre's analysis of the contradictions of the built environment reveal the city in its complexity as what he calls a "space of differences."[2] This space is a field in tension, which includes nature, as evident in his definition of social space as the "encounter, assembly, [and] simultaneity...of everything that is produced by nature or by society, either through their cooperation or through their conflicts."[3] This vision of a city pursues relationships between social and natural forces acknowledging disturbances and denying to any one force complete control over the other.

How does a designer embrace that which s/he cannot control, including the agency of individuals in terms of how they might envision themselves in a space or appropriate it for unplanned uses, in order to contribute to the longer or fuller life of a space? One approach to this challenge is through the construction of a spatial heterogeneity, which can support or bring about change within itself. Vito Acconci's juxtaposition of playground and theater helps to construct the dynamic identity of Island in the Mur. The disturbance of one space by another becomes part of an ecosystem of public spaces, with the potential to produce an energy that is more than the sum of its parts. Such a precise activation of difference recalls Acconci's performative approach to gallery installations in his work as an artist.

The ability of a project to operate in terms that acknowledge and facilitate difference can be enhanced by understanding how different functions operate at different scales, in order to overlay and construct links between them. Island in the Mur is a fantasy space– the ultimate nonfunctional destination, yet it also has a multifunctional, multi-scalar identity, including as a bridge and as a performance space. Because of the river's history as a divider of the two sides of the city, its crossing is a significant urban event, bringing together different socioeconomic groups in flows which interact with Island in the Mur's local activities. Acconci constructs the island's paradoxical identity as new city center and irreducible other place by alternating between affiliation and differentiation: situating the stepped amphitheater so that it seems to become a part of the sloping terrain of the city beyond, while aligning the island's longitudinal axis with the flow of water to emphasize its autonomy from the historically divided urban landscape.

The hybrid identity of Carme Pinós' fairground-park also reflects an attention to adjacencies. Conceived as part of an urban experiment, it operates in a way that overlaps its own physical boundaries in relation to neighboring programs, including the convention center, shopping, amphitheater, and hotel. The project's identity is both clarified and layered as it opens up to these other precincts as prospect and place, and also operates as a threshold between them and the existing national park. Pinós articulates the project's hybridity in ribbon-like forms that repeat at different scales and across different uses: the arc of the pedestrian bridges parallels that of the stalls in plan and section. Multiplied and brought together in changing compositions, these architectural elements are woven into and become part of the ground, with the ground in turn becoming architecture over a relatively large area. Pinós traverses a line between architecture and landscape so often that architecture begins to function as a field condition at a scale associated with that of a landscape. The project's dynamic formal language supports movement, in a way that is assisted programmatically by enabling pauses: the field is punctuated with shaded areas, where, as ground comes up and transforms into small structures, vegetation will follow it, providing respite in the hot climate, to create a more desirable place to walk.

In the development of urban space, a broad definition of program as inhabitation is more effective than a narrow definition in terms of use. Inhabitation in this sense has to do with a person's ability to map where s/he is, in order to construct a position. The concept of positioning touches on Frederic Jameson's discussion of cognitive mapping, a term he takes from Kevin Lynch, and develops as a response to what he identifies as alienation in the face of new urban geographies. Cognitive mapping is about establishing a relationship with something other. According to this framework, a project's program may include the reinterpretation of a site's contradictions in a way that does not neutralize them, as well as providing a mechanism for individuals to map themselves in relation to such contradictory presences.

The Mori Art Museum offers residents and visitors a position in the city that they could not have imagined before. To occupy this position makes it possible to map oneself in relation to the new and unfamiliar urban geography of Roppongi Hills. In the design of the museum, the architect Richard Gluckman focuses on positioning as both program and strategy. As a visitor emerges from the elevator on the 52nd floor of the tower, uninterrupted views across the museum's double-level central atrium orient her/him simultaneously within the galleries and in reference to the building's perimeter, which is encircled by a continuous promenade with an upper level gallery. The promenade represents a common thread among the five projects that is related to positioning, which is the use of movement as a way to simultaneously function as and represent urban space. In this case, the promenade asserts the importance of an outward focus on the urban landscape as a parallel to the inward focus of the gallery spaces. A mirrored and angled canopy heightens and multiplies the visibility of the city as a landscape which includes the building, allowing an individual to simultaneously inhabit the building and the city. This transformation of city into landscape in visual terms engages landscape in new paradoxical ways, while playing on historical conventions. As well as offering a means of positioning oneself within Roppongi Hills' new geography, the museum functions as an icon helping to define it. Year-round every-evening programming supports its appearance as a lit platform floating above the dark office tower, its displaced ground representing a new kind of public space.

The design of Westergasfabriek Park also constructs the possibility for a new position, by inscribing a space of inhabitation into an industrial landscape of disused gas cylinders. Kathryn Gustafson combines multiple scales within the project, a refusal to domesticate this landscape that is so out of scale with the human body. In addition to the gas cylinders, one of which is remade as a theater, the park has large spaces that operate at scales that are conventionally associated with landscape, in terms of ecological processes and types of connections, as well as artists' studios, exhibition halls, and smaller outdoor spaces, that function at scales more often associated with architecture. In this park landscape is program, not in a pastoral tradition of refuge, which requires extensive space to reproduce an apparent wholeness of nature, or the tradition of City Beautiful, which reduces landscape to polite background. Instead, landscape as process is conceived as part of the city as a space of (incommensurable) differences. Gustafson represents such ideological shifts by tracing their history in a succession of new uses and experiences in the intervening space between the existing eighteenth-century Westerpark and her transformation of its previously industrial neighbor. This spatial progression represents changing attitudes towards landscape, in order to acknowledge it as a cultural construction, but also strives, through its arrival at spaces which are a result of a present-day process of reclamation, to integrate humans into an ecologically-based understanding of the land.

The forms of the South-East Coastal Park and Auditoriums, also a brownfield site, are driven not only by Foreign Office Architects' desire to make a compelling landscape in visual terms but also by the need to create a pedestrian connection from the city to the waterfront swimming platform. This creates an interface between the different ground levels. FOA deploys figural qualities conventionally associated with landscape to configure the ground as spaces to sit, be sheltered, walk, accommodate planting, and so on. These spaces are worked into the urban landscape in a way that is less total than in FOA's Yokohama Port Terminal project, which is also conceived and modeled in landscape terms. The coastal park is more flexible construction, alternately adhering to, thickening, or fragmenting the land/water edge to make it into a place to inhabit. The project covers an existing treatment plant with a new concrete ground plane made up of varied and sometimes multi-layered surfaces. These surfaces share a vocabulary in which contours define a dune-like landscape, that is then flattened out in places to make a super graphic pattern on the ground, which opens up to become seating and support for other social uses. It also operates as an infrastructure for nature to support reeds, grass and trees.

Several projects in the exhibition invest in spaces for an event that has always occurred but because of its transience has not been considered an appropriate subject for design. Historically, an event such as Guadalajara's October Feast would be supported by a blank slate, upon which the fair's infrastructure would be mounted and demounted. Pinós not only designs spaces for the festival; she represents its temporality in traces that encourage other movements during the remainder of the year. This new way of thinking about program acknowledges that space is not universal. By envisioning the stands empty or sporadically inhabited at certain times of year, as well as fully occupied at others, Pinós makes two or more different landscapes. The articulation of the architectural elements as emergent rather than for instance separate, allows the field to shift registers between its several identities. When it is empty of the goods and services associated with the festival, it becomes a different, equally remarkable public space, and not merely the abandoned shell of activities that happen at a more important time of year.

Just as insights into ecosystem dynamics have shown that many future scenarios are possible for the ecological development of a site, the same is true for program. The sustained existence of Island in the Mur, built as a temporary project, was neither an *a priori* condition of its realization, nor a fortuitous accident, but instead the result of a willingness to invest in something with an uncertain outcome. In identifying design frameworks that might facilitate such an investment without resorting to an "anything goes" open-endedness, the most compelling examples are to be found in innovative contemporary landscape architectural design practices, which are engaging ecological systems to develop mutable but still precise frameworks that can manage complexity and embrace change within the structure of a project.

The landscape ecologist and planner Nina-Marie Lister has outlined a concept of adaptive design, which is based on the complex ecological systems for which it is a decision making model. As she defines it, adaptive design is flexible in the sense of being context-dependent, process based and resilient.[4] This framework can help to conceptualize projects in terms of their cultural as well as natural sustainability, and programmatic as well as ecological resilience. Lister's framework is notable for the way in which it crosses between science and value systems, social and ecological orders, to outline an integrated approach that does not seek wholeness, eschewing control and certainty for resonance.

The willingness of designers to handle increased temporal and spatial programmatic complexity and/or instability reflects digital technology's capacity to layer and manage information. Contemporary modes of research and representation in the design of public spaces often rely on a matrix, which supports articulation of a project's identity as a complex weave rather than a singular whole. The design of each of the five new meeting grounds projects entails orchestration of a matrix of operations at different scales in space and time.[5] It is through such a matrix that a project can be designed to serve a precise set of programmatic needs, and at the same time to exceed this set of needs in order to sustain a longer life or serve a larger sphere. Such a matrix facilitates the engagement of temporality in both cultural and natural processes, making it possible to envision a project in terms of its difference in space and time.

[1] Gilles Deleuze, *The Logic of Sense*, V. Boundas (Ed.), Translated by Mark Lester with Charles Stivale (New York: Columbia University Press, 1990): 77

[2] Henri Lefebvre, *The Production of Space*, Translated by Donald Nicholson-Smith (Oxford: Blackwell Publishers, 1991): 101

[3] Ibid: 101

[4] Nina Marie Lister, "Adaptive Design," presented at the Large Parks Symposium, Harvard Design School, April 2003. Additional relevant characteristics of this "new" ecology include the regular emergence of new functions, the presence of biodiversity to ensure renewal, and the dominance of cycling and feedback over linear cause and effect.

[5] See Anita Berrizbeitia and Linda Pollak, "Operations between Architecture and Landscape," in *Inside Outside: Between Architecture and Landscape* (Rockport Publications, 1999): 10-13

ACTIVE
MEMORY

Memorials have been located in the center of cities for millennia, even when the cemeteries themselves were outside the city walls, yet the way we understand and use memory as part of civic life continues to evolve. After 9/11, New York questioned whether the most significant memorial would be rebuilding what was lost, and more broadly, reviving Lower Manhattan, or by contrast, to leave the entire site vacant. In between, where current policy lies, involves ideas of a place of reflection, programs roughly corresponding to a "living memorial" (culture, education), and commercial revival. Many decisions have been made, but the ultimate role of memory downtown, and for history in cities around the world, is far from decided.

Three projects address memory very differently: one a 4.9-acre site to the murdered Jews of Europe in **Berlin, Germany;** another a large square dedicated to one of the founding sites of a renewed nation in **Kliptown, in the Soweto township in Johannesburg, South Africa,** now memorializing Walter Sisulu, one of the founders and great leaders of the African National Congress for half a century; and another a pedestrian bridge dedicated to those lost in the break-up of the former Yugoslavia in **Rijeka, Croatia.** In summary, these are: a memorial precinct, an active multi-use square, and a busy bridge, with events to be remembered ranging from horror and oppression to liberation and freedom. In South Africa and Croatia infrastructure projects (a square, a bridge) serve both commemorative events and quotidian purposes of getting from here to there, shopping, and meeting. In Berlin, the memorial is deliberately not part of the infrastructure of the city. To the degree that it becomes a site for events, they will connect to its core memorial function, and while its "field" organization strives against the closed systems of many traditional memorials, it seems impossible for its identity to fade into the background. Yet what will a 25-year-old in 2025 feel? Set between Berlin's "Central Park" in the center of a thriving city, and major commercial developments, this memorial like those in Croatia, South Africa, and New York will ultimately be both "other" and part of the urban everyday.

MEMORIAL FOR THE MURDERED JEWS OF EUROPE

BERLIN, GERMANY
EISENMAN ARCHITECTS

OVERVIEW

Architect Peter Eisenman's monumental design for a Memorial for the Murdered Jews of Europe reinterprets traditional commemorative schemes. At the scale of a park, the design is a public space that is planned to be open and experienced 24 hours a day. Under construction on the 4.9-acre former site of the Ministry Gardens located between the Brandenburg Gate and Hitler's bunker during World War II, in central Berlin, the memorial is a landscape of columns set 37 inches apart so that individuals can walk between them. The winning entry in an international design competition spearheaded by the then-Chancellor Helmut Kohl in 1997, the memorial honors the six million Jews who were victims of the National Socialist Regime.

DESIGNER

Peter Eisenman, whose firm Eisenman Architects, based in New York, won the international competition to build the memorial in 1999, is known for his theoretical work, teaching and writing as much as for his architecture. Founder of the Institute for Architecture and Urban Studies in 1967 and director until 1982, Eisenman established his office in 1980. His work includes The Wexner Center for the Visual Arts and Fine Arts Library, social housing at Checkpoint Charlie, along the Berlin Wall and the City of Culture of Galicia (CCG), Spain planned to be completed in 2004.

DESCRIPTION

The memorial consists of 2,700 concrete pillars, each two meters wide and seven meters tall, arranged in a grid, on an undulating site slightly below street level. The irregular landscape that gently rises and falls up to seven feet in certain places will create the effect of a rippling field of stones. A 5,600-square-foot single level multi-media research center, the Ort, with a symbolic wall of one million books will be set below ground under the southeast corner. Visitors can enter the site from all four sides at any point and enter the Ort via stairs or a ramp that slips down between the stones.

PROCESS

The idea for a Memorial for the Murdered Jews of Europe was conceived of in 1988 by a group led by journalist Lea Rosh and the historian Eberhard Jaeckel. Slowly garnering public support over the next decade, in 1992, three years af-

ter the fall of the wall and one year after the government's decision to make Berlin the capital of the reunited Germany, Chancellor Helmut Kohl resolved to support the project. Ten years on, and the memorial has proven to be a contentious issue that has gone through various iterations, including two international design competitions.

In 1994, Chancellor Kohl announced the first competition to be steered by a Findungskommission who were responsible for shaping the decision-making process. The members were professors Christoph Stoezl, Dieter Ronte, James E. Young, Werner Hofmann and Josef Paul Kleihues. 528 submissions were received from which artist Christine Jackob-Marks' design was chosen in 1995. Her proposal featured an almost 108,000 square foot concrete slab engraved with the names of the 4.2 million Jews identified by the Yad Vashem Holocaust Memorial in Israel. A public debate ensued driven by criticism that the scheme was too grandiose and threatened the two million unidentified Jews with anonymity, leading to Chancellor Kohl's rejection of the design. In 1997 a second competition was held amid controversy over the size of the site allocated to the memorial. Opinions ranged from the memorial being unnecessary in a city that already has a number of smaller memorials to others believing it necessary for the city to confront this chapter in its history. In 1998 four finalists' projects were chosen including a grid of 4,000 concrete columns measuring up to 13 feet in height by Peter Eisenman and artist Richard Serra.

In 1999, after several public hearings and presentations of the designs, Eisenman and Serra's proposal was announced the winner. However, in a response to critics who found the scheme too stylized and ahistorical, Chancellor Kohl and cultural minister Michael Naumann asked that the design be scaled back to 2,700 columns and that a research center, later called the Ort, be added. This decision prompted Serra to pull out of the design. Eisenman proceeded.

OUTLOOK

The memorial, bordered by a major road and the Tiergarten to the west and embassies and the Headquarters of DG Bank by Frank O. Gehry to the north, is situated in an area that already draws heavy traffic from locals and tourists alike. Eisenman's design is set to become a destination in itself.

*View of model of the Memorial for the Murdered Jews of Europe,
looking northeast*

"Remembering the Holocaust can only be a living condition in which the past remains active in the present. In this memorial, there is no nostalgia, no memory of the past, only the living memory of the individual experience."

PETER EISENMAN,
EISENMAN ARCHITECTS

"Eisenman is not answering the question of Germany's dilemma—how does a nation commemorate those murdered in its name—but rather is articulating this dilemma in the design in a way that he hopes will be indeterminate. There are as many ways into this memorial as there are entries on the grid, and then there are also numberless ways through this memorial: everyone will create their own path in memory."

JAMES E. YOUNG,
PROFESSOR OF ENGLISH AND
JUDAIC STUDIES AT THE UNIVERSITY
OF MASSACHUSETTS AT AMHERST

"The design of an open memorial space, accessible all day and night to everybody presents a new type of memorial and makes the necessary experience of commemoration a social experience."

GÜNTER SCHLUSCHE,
STIFTUNG DENKMAL FÜR DIE
ERMORDETEN JUDEN EUROPAS

MEMORIAL BRIDGE

RIJEKA, CROATIA
3LHD

OVERVIEW

The Memorial Bridge in the center of the City of Rijeka, on Croatia's northern coastline, completed in 2001 is both a practical piece of infrastructure connecting the east and west sides of the city as well as an act of commemoration. The bridge, which spans the Rijecina Canal, honors the Croatian soldiers who departed from the Delta district located at the west juncture of the bridge and were killed in the civil wars of the 1990s.

DESIGNERS

In 1997 the city council held a competition for a bridge to connect Delta, an area to the west, left abandoned since the decline of the docks, and more recently used as a car park, and the old historical center of the city to the east. The competition brief also called for a memorial either on the bridge or beside it. The winning design is by Zagreb-based architecture office 3LHD, founded in 1994 and headed by Silvije Novak, Marko Dabrovic, Sasa Begovic, and Tanja Grozdanic, graduates from the University of Zagreb. The firm, which has since won numerous awards for their design, focuses its practice on projects that integrate architecture, art and the urban landscape.

DESCRIPTION

From the start of the project, 3LHD resolved to create a bridge that would both function as an elegant connecting device for the two sides of the city as well as be a memorial. The simple design consists of a plank over the canal terminating at two slabs driven into the ground. The bridge spans 150 feet, 123 feet over the water. Its minimal design language is the result of the ingenuity of its design and engineering. 3LHD approached the project with a three-fold wish list: to create a bridge that was as thin as possible; to use an homogenous material for the decking over the water and the vertical columns, and to illuminate the bridge without a visible light source.

Working with structural engineers CES to achieve their goals, 3LHD developed a self-supporting structure made from concrete 18 feet wide and 2 feet thick held rigid by hollow steel girders that continue into the banks of the river. Both the bridge and the 30-foot-tall columns are clad in panels made from an alloy, invented specifically for this project, of aluminum and magnesium. The columns are further detailed with a three-foot-high transparent glass top. A railing made from sheets of 3/4-inch-thick toughened glass topped with a round-edged teak handrail frames the edges of the bridge. LEDs embedded into the underside of the handrail illuminate the footbridge at night with an even light and create a seamless light source that doesn't interrupt the sleek design. LEDs have also been sunk into the ground between the two columns to delineate the cleft between them, which has symbolic value, and are positioned under the cantilevered teak benches in Delta Square. The benches mimic the simple form and the orientation of the bridge. The 150-ton construction was built in the local 3 Maj shipyard and shipped by sea. A barge was specially designed that would be able to sail under two existing bridges. Once it arrived at Delta, the kit of parts was then assembled on site.

OUTLOOK

The Memorial Bridge does more than act as a commemorative walkway, its monumental design defines the public space around it. Approaching from the east, a narrow pathway made of red clay and epoxy, delineates the route to the bridge, terminating at the base of the columns. From the west, the bridge connects to a pedestrian crossing and Korzo, the main street in the city that connects to the car park soon to be transformed into a park. In a single defining gesture, 3LHD have contributed to Rijeka's identity by creating an iconic L-shaped bridge and a memorable spatial experience.

View of the Memorial Bridge, over the Rijecina Canal, Rijeka, Croatia, looking west. The bridge honors the Croatian soldiers of the 1990s civil wars

PHOTO: ALJOSA BRAJDIC,
DAMIR FABIJANIC, 3LHD

"The task we set ourselves was to make a structure that would dominate the area, while at the same time awaken an intimate feeling—that is to create a monument for walking on. At the same time we wanted to foster public interaction in the area and create a meeting place."

3LHD

"The proportions of the bridge and the materials used create a totally intimate perception of the space, almost as if an interior has for some reason found itself in the open. The physical particularity of crossing the bridge is heightened by the aluminum planks which produce a distinctive sound while walking."

SASA RANDIC
ORIS MAGAZINE FOR ARCHITECTURE AND CULTURE

WALTER SISULU SQUARE OF DEDICATION

OVERVIEW

There is currently no marker to symbolize the historic Congress of the People, held on June 26, 1955, on an open piece of land that became known as Freedom Square in Johannesburg, South Africa. Celebrating this momentous occasion with a monument, as well as defining a central gathering space were among the goals of the Freedom Square open, national design competition organized in 2002.

The competition was won by the Johannesburg firm studioMAS Architecture and Urban Design. At the unveiling of the design the square was renamed Walter Sisulu Square of Dedication in honor of the former Deputy President of the ANC. Sisulu, one of the great historic leaders of South Africa, died in May 2003. The project is part of the Local Integrated Development Plan to regenerate Soweto and the City of Johannesburg through an urban planning, design and development program. The design for the square has been allocated a budget of approximately $15 million. The broader budget for the area around the square is $50 million.

DESIGNERS

studioMAS was established in 2000 by Pierre Swanepoel. Precious Makwe and Justin Snell are project team members. Recent projects include the Villa Bazaruto in Mozambique, and writing the Manual for Sustainable Urban Development for the South African Government.

BACKGROUND

Soweto, a township within the City of Johannesburg, has a population of more than one million, half of whom are under the age of 25, and an area of 95 square miles. Soweto contains 43% of the population of the City of Johannesburg, and, was historically the largest black township. Kliptown, established in 1903 was one of the first townships in which blacks could own property. It is best known as the site of the Congress of the People, initiated by Professor Z. K. Matthews and members of the African National Congress in 1955. Over 2,800 elected delegates and 7,000 spectators gathered to hear and comment on the draft of the Freedom Charter. The Charter formulated a vision of a time "when all South Africans will live and work together, without racial bitterness and fear of misery, in peace and harmony."

DESCRIPTION

Walter Sisulu Square of Dedication, presently an unkempt piece of land of roughly two acres, is situated directly east of the Soweto Commuter Railway line and the Klipspruit River and wetlands. It is a thriving trading area characterized by the makeshift market stalls to the east of the square, which lie behind Union Street, Kliptown's main shopping center. The competition for the square was open-ended and called for competitors to write their own briefs. In keeping with the participatory nature of the 1955 Congress, a community liaison group presented the 34 competition entries to the public.

studioMAS approached their design with three basic premises: "designing an appropriately monumental and decorous place; acknowledging the history and memory of the event and the site; and creating a vibrant place of intense economic and cultural activity." These were then addressed by nine key principles (symbolizing the nine provinces) that became a value system that anchored the design: Equity, Identity, Vitality, Accessibility, History, Legibility, Symbolism, Ecology, and Robustness. Two large squares make up the design; one represents the old apartheid South Africa and the other represents the new, democratic South Africa. The "old" square is the original site of the Congress. Left open for large gatherings, the square will have a stage at its west side for meetings and concerts and a new market area to the south with 600 stalls for traders.

The "new" square to the east of the site will be defined by a grid of nine squares each marked by a cross made from stones brought in by people from the nine provinces, signifying the votes cast in the country's first democratic elections in 1994. An auditorium, exhibition space, museum and the monument will be placed on this square. A pathway of trees divides the two major squares and leads to the monument at the north. The monument is a 50-foot-high conical tower illuminated by an eternal flame at its center and with an "X" cut into its roof marking freedom.

OUTLOOK

The bold design that accommodates intimate and large scale gathering spaces resonates with symbolic and historical references but at the same time stands as a symbol of Kliptown's urban revitalization. As well as by a monument, the design celebrates freedom and opportunity by generating income for the community.

View of Walter Sisulu Square of Dedication, Kliptown, Johannesburg,
South Africa, showing covered marketplace

RENDERING: FORESIGHT ANIMATION

Aerial view of Walter Sisulu Square
of Dedication

RENDERING: FORESIGHT ANIMATION

"The square has been designed as an open public 'room' in the city."

STUDIOMAS ARCHITECTURE AND URBAN DESIGN

"The scheme provides a strategy to begin a process of transformation of ex-urban settlements like Soweto into more urbane places. While resolving the issues of the competition site and its memorialization, this project went on to demonstrate how infrastructural elements such as avenues, squares, arcades, parks, and denser development could be introduced into these sprawling worlds, and despite modest means such as landscape and trees, have significant effect."

STANLEY SAITOWITZ, CHAIR,
JURY FOR THE FREEDOM SQUARE
ARCHITECTURAL COMPETITION

"The project was chosen for its bold scale and also for its exemplary potential to change Soweto into a city... the elements suggested in the design are not revolutionary—they are traditional ingredients of urban space—but in the context of Soweto, they became radical in establishing a place as significant as Central Park is to New York, or the mall to Washington, or the ceremonial spaces are of emerging cities like Brasilia or Chandigarh."

REPORT BY THE JURY FOR THE
FREEDOM SQUARE ARCHITECTURAL
COMPETITION

MEMORY
WORK

Marc Kristal is a journalist and
screenwriter with a special
interest in architecture, design
and urbanism. He is the curator
of "Absence Into Presence:
The Art, Architecture and Design
of Remembrance," on view at
Parsons School of Design in
fall 2003

'We should ask to what end we have remembered. That is, how do we respond to the
current moment in light of the remembered past? This is to recognize that the shape of
memory cannot be divorced from actions taken on its behalf, and that memory without
consequences contains the seeds of its own destruction.'

James E. Young, *The Texture of Memory: Holocaust Memorials and Meaning* (Yale University Press, 1993)

As James Young's observation suggests, the work of memory demands, not only that we
honor events and individuals, but that we come to the right conclusions about the past
and put them to meaningful use in our own time. From the standpoint of urban design,
this would seem to involve the creation of remembrances that, like cities, remain alive and
mutable—remembrances that recognize that the past is ever-present while enabling us to
use that knowledge to build a better tomorrow.

Designing the memory of the past into the future life of the city, however, is a tricky
business, due not only to the twin complexities of remembrance design and urbanism,
but to the nature of memory itself. Broadly speaking, there are two kinds of memory
relevant to the subject. The first is public, our collective knowledge of the sites and events
that comprise the history of a city, as well as the emotional consensus that hangs over
each (i.e., that happened there and that was tragic). The second kind of memory involves
the intimate lives of a city's inhabitants: the private recollections sparked by the constant
interplay between an individual consciousness and the urban environment—what might
be called Proustian memory (i.e., the aroma of that hot dog stand reminds me of my first
love).

Traditionally, the products of remembrance design have spoken mostly to public
memory, in the language of the official monument—a statue, a memorial structure of
some sort, a building or public square named for an illustrious citizen. This can be detrimental both to cities and to memory-work, as public memory tends to be fixed in meaning and time (and thus a poor contributor to the present), and the remembrances that
result from it invariably relieve a city's citizens of the job of having to act on the lessons of
the past. Such remembrances can be as dead as the people and events they honor and, as
they do our work for us (and often not very well), contribute little to the present or future
of any city.

Part of the problem—and it is a subtle one—is that, by paying insufficient attention to
the role that private memory plays in our daily lives, artists, architects and planners dealing with remembrance often end up divorcing it from the human requirements of use.
While no one would design a park or transportation system without considering the effects of things like noise, comfort and accessibility on the end user, comparable attention
is seldom paid to what might be called the ergonomics of memory, the palpable systemic

effects produced by that interplay between remembrance of things past and present-time experience. This is unfortunate, because memory is embedded in the nerves and senses as much as it is in facts—indeed, it is in the moment, and not the past, that memory lives.

Thus the most effective examples of remembrance in urban life are ones that engage both public and private memory—works that, though they deal with historical events, remain connected to the ongoing narrative of the city by provoking the personal connections that unite our outer and inner lives. Because we take them personally, such remembrances are at once less likely to lose meaning over time, and more helpful in terms of bringing to bear the lessons of history on the present.

The latter may be especially significant when considering projects that deal with the Holocaust. Incorporating remembrances of one of history's most unspeakable horrors into the active life of a city is difficult for many reasons, and nowhere more so than in Germany, where the work of remembering falls upon the perpetrators and their descendants. Yet the German situation is precisely the sort that demands the kind of active (as opposed to ossified) remembrance on which the life of a city is built, and just such a memorial was created by Israeli artist Micha Ullman for Bebelplatz, an 18th-century square in the center of Berlin. In 1933, Bebelplatz was the site of an infamous, Nazi-orchestrated book burning, during which some 20,000 volumes were fed to the flames. Ullman's work leaves nothing on view in the square except a small transparent pane set into the cobblestones. Visible beneath it is a chamber filled with empty shelves—enough to hold 20,000 books. A plaque offers a quote from Heine: "When books are burned, in the end people will burn."

Coming upon Ullman's installation is like stepping on a mnemonic rake: one receives a deracinating jolt that conflates present and past, and even puts one uncomfortably in the shoes of the perpetrators. The work does this, moreover, with only the most minimal intervention into the urban fabric. Indeed, it is the visitor—who, peering through the glass and experiencing a mix of personal and historical associations, thinks Never Again—who is the monument. Rather than being "finished," Ullman's piece is reborn every time someone sees it. Like such provocative Holocaust memorials as Rachel Whiteread's Nameless Library and Jochen and Esther Gerz's Monument against Fascism, Bebelplatz contributes to the urban present by fighting nostalgia and heightening perception.

Peter Eisenman's Memorial for the Murdered Jews of Europe, too, is anti-nostalgic, and invites the visitor to create a unique experience in space and time, one that will express, as the architect puts it, "the idea that all closed systems of a closed order are bound to fail." Yet, as an abstract expression of a generality about totalitarianism, the memorial reflects its role as Germany's "official" (read final) word on one of history's greatest crimes; and by turning it very obviously into a "destination," the work's size and location may paradoxically make it easier to avoid. (Time, of course, will tell.)

The challenges of acceptance Eisenman's project will face remind us that, while a discrete memorial must attract an audience, active memory can be woven into a city's life via its infrastructure. In fact, one of the most satisfying Holocaust remembrances, Karin Daan's Homomonument, takes the form of a pink stone triangle that steps down from the sidewalk and juts discreetly into Amsterdam's Keizergracht Canal. This small "sitting pier," which evokes the pink triangle the Nazis forced homosexuals to wear on their sleeves—and was later subverted by the gay pride movement into a symbol of resistance—effectively converts what was first a badge of shame, then of honor, into a part of everyday life.

Remembrance-by-infrastructure, as Daan's project demonstrates, represents a different kind of challenge—how can memory be organically worked into the utilitarian?—one met eloquently by 3LHD's Memorial Bridge in Rijeka, Croatia. The architects have elevated a simple footbridge into a meditation on life's beauty and fragility, in part by incorporating water—the Rijecina Canal, which flows beneath it—into the experience.

The use of natural elements in remembrance design has its roots in antiquity; fire, water, smoke, even the earth itself bestow a sense of the eternal, while also imparting an awareness of transformation between states of being. Water is a particularly satisfying memorial element, for its multiple associations, the quality of the sound it produces and the opportunity it offers for participation. In her 1988 Civil Rights Memorial, for example, Maya Lin was inspired to include water by a line from Dr. Martin Luther King Jr.'s "I Have a Dream" speech: "We are not satisfied and will not be satisfied until justice rolls down like waters and righteousness like a mighty stream." Lin created a "water table," featuring a time line of significant events in the history of the civil rights movement, including forty deaths. And at the memorial's dedication, Lin witnessed an act of participation, when the mother of murdered teenager Emmett Till touched her son's name beneath the moving water, and let her tears fall into it.

On the Memorial Bridge, pedestrians interact with the water through its meaning and sound. The thinness of the metal decking, as well as the transparent glass railing, contrive to create a "room" that seems to float in space, hanging improbably above the moving water (with its associations of journeying, cleansing and healing). The water's sound increases awareness of it, as does the contrasting report of heels echoing on the metal. This combination of "hard" and "soft" sounds heightens the perception of life as a room entered only for a time—one that hangs above the void—and reminds the walker of the memorial's purpose: to honor the soldiers who left from the western juncture of the bridge to die in the Balkan wars of the 1990s. The architects draw pedestrians into an otherworldly zone—and from there into memory—before delivering them, on the other side, back to life.

If embedding remembrance in the infrastructure is one way of making it an organic part of the urban landscape, another involves using the past, quite literally, to create the future, as a tool of urban renewal. This is the strategy behind Walter Sisulu Square of Dedication in Kliptown, a district within the Soweto township of Johannesburg. Here, the desire to begin the conversion of an exurban, haphazardly developed yet populous and culturally significant area into an urbane part of a modern city happily coincided with the fact that one of modern South Africa's most important events took place there. Thus can the district's developers use an important component of both public and private memory —pride in the history and accomplishments of one's people—to drive the project's design and help to ensure its success.

The role of memory is important as well to the long-term ambitions for Kliptown and Soweto. In their "Vision & Delivery framework" document, studioMAS, the firm responsible for the square's design, notes that the objective is "a vibrant environment where people feel comfortable and safe to live, work and visit"—i.e., success depends in part upon a setting in which the area's vitality is retained but the perception of danger is diminished. Toward this end, studioMAS has elegantly infused its plan for this multi-use zone, which will include a major transit hub and market stalls among other economic and infrastructural components, with references not only to the struggle against apartheid and the Congress of the People, but to the importance of unity, democracy and responsibility. One imagines that, surrounded by memories of South Africa's heroes, their labors, and the values that helped them triumph, visitors to Walter Sisulu Square as well as the residents of Kliptown and Soweto will feel a more personal commitment to the development's success.

It is tempting, when considering the Soweto project, to wonder if it offers any lessons to the developers of the World Trade Center site. The twin towers, after all, represented an urban renewal effort, one that began with the rejuvenation and expansion of Manhattan's financial district, and evolved in the course of a generation into a vital new quarter of New York City. The redesign and rebuilding of the Trade Center site also represents an opportunity for urban renewal: to correct the earlier design's infrastructural limitations, create cultural institutions where none existed, to improve the neighborhood's architecture. As with Walter Sisulu Square, remembrance is the design's driving force; unlike the

Soweto project, which will be built on the triumph of justice over inhumanity, the new World Trade Center will be permeated with the memory of one of the worst tragedies in American history.

As in lower Manhattan, there will be a memorial element in Soweto. But what is striking about Sisulu Square is the way in which memory has been designed into all of its elements, and it is this that perhaps offers something to the Trade Center mandarins. With his sublime instinct for symbolism, Daniel Libeskind, principal architect of the site, has grasped that, in the bedrock left where the towers once stood, we already have a surpassing remembrance: here the towers fell, taking lives and the confidence of the American Century with them; here as well, the retaining walls held, men and women cleared the rubble and removed the dead, here we endured. Libeskind has made the bedrock the cornerstone of his scheme, and one hopes that the simple eloquence of this idea will find its way into every aspect of what is built—that memory will not be limited to a few public, monumental gestures, general and sentimental, that lock the new development inexorably in the past.

Long after the last South African with a living memory of Walter Sisulu is gone, people will walk through his square and experience the interplay of public and private remembrance in a way that will let them look forward while looking back. Equally, one hopes that, when all the survivors and families of the dead of 9/11 are gone, when the event has passed into history, what is built in lower Manhattan will engage the active memory of future visitors, and enable them to move forward—that the role memory plays will rescue the history of 9/11 from the tragedy of loss, and return it to the pride of endurance.

TEMP WORK

Zoë Ryan

Since the "happenings" of the 1960s, artists, architects, landscape architects, and designers of all kinds have continued to demonstrate how temporary interventions can permanently alter our perception of public space. The most compelling are orchestrated to be experiences: environments in which visitors are immersed, whether on a literally physical level through built structures or more viscerally through movement, sound, and light in a performance. The projects included here are just a few examples and involve media technologies, constructed environments, dance, even a table set with food. They have all had a powerful impact on changing expectations of what can happen in public. These works last as long as six months, a matter of days or no more than 24 hours. All of them are meant to be received as explorations, prompting new readings and interpretations and energizing our relationship to public space.

View of Tribute in Light,
September 11, 2003

PHOTO: JONATHAN COHEN-LITANT

At their most dramatic, interventions can play out at the scale of the city. The poignant Tribute in Light commemorating the events of September 11th was conceived by John Bennett and Gustavo Bonevardi of PROUN Space Studio, artists Julian LaVerdiere and Paul Myoda, architect Richard Nash Gould, and lighting designer Paul Marantz and organized by the Municipal Art Society and Creative Time. "In a very direct and genuine way, temporary interventions remind us that change is possible, that the world is not fixed, that individuals can make a difference, and that there are ways of looking at the world in new and unexpected ways," says Tom Eccles, Executive Director of the Public Art Fund in New York. "In that sense, these projects, even if they are not strictly political in nature, are a fundamental assertion of democracy and tolerance."

Public Space has often been referred to as a stage on which the everyday is acted. For the past two years, the theatricality of the Parisian urban experience has been heightened by Paris Plage, a two mile-long "seaside" installed for July and August on the Georges Pompidou expressway that runs along the river Seine. For a number of years the expressways along the Seine had been closed to traffic for a few weeks in July and August so that residents could enjoy the river free of cars. Prompted by the popularity of these open days, Mayor Bertrand Delanoë hired "scenographer" Jean-Christophe Choblet to rethink the nature of this road and create a provisional parkway that could be assembled on site and dismantled at the end of the summer.

At a cost of approximately $1 million, 17 city agencies installed an almost 350-foot-long sand beach with 80 imported palm trees, 22 blue and white striped changing tents, 150 parasols and 300 blue canvas deckchairs. They added grass lawns, water sprinklers, boules pitches, a platform for dancing and other areas for concerts. Additional features of the project were a rock climbing wall, a river fishing club, a play area for children, a marine-knot-tying clinic and a skate and roller rental outlet, and two walls for graffiti artists to tag. Open 24 hours a day free of charge, the beach attracted over three million visitors. This year the project was more ambitious, incorporating an additional beach area, a series of water features as well as street furniture and it is set to take on even more functions next year. Choblet explains that his goal was to "produce a public space that had a mix of social uses for every sector of the population of Paris and beyond." Calling his projects "urban scenography," Choblet works to integrate visitors into the scene. He contributes to the cinematic perception of these stage-like settings by considering every detail from the sound of the landscape, the quality of materials employed to the humidity levels. His aim is to encourage viewer participation and remove us from our everyday environment. In this way he illustrates the possibilities for multiple experiences inherent in public space.

Paris Plage was a city-sponsored project. Elsewhere cultural institutions have established architectural programs to commission venues for events that mediate between the interior and exterior spaces. For example, the MoMA/P.S.1 Young Architects Forum selects a team of designers to transform the courtyard of P.S.1 in Long Island City. 2003 was the fourth year of the Forum. In 2003, Los Angeles-based Emergent designed an urban beachscape for the summer, incorporating a stage to host a weekly music series. In previous years local firms SHoP and ROY were selected.

Concepts in architectural design have been traditionally communicated through exhibitions featuring drawings, models, photographs and computer renderings. Built structures provide an additional provocative means to investigate possibilities. Garofolo Architects took this idea and in 2003 built an installation for the plaza in front of the Museum of Contemporary Art (MCA). Commissioned by Elizabeth Smith, MCA's James W. Alsdorf Chief Curator, she says the project "enabled the plaza to be transformed and encouraged occupation—rather than just being used as a passageway through to somewhere else."

Lise-Anne Couture, a partner at Asymptote, claims such structures have an important advantage over models and drawings. "Often temporary installations can be more experimental because they can operate around building codes." In 1996, this New-York based architecture firm created a temporary 30,000 square foot multi-media installation in Bispertov Square for the Aarhus Theater Festival in Denmark. Couture praises the benefits of ephemeral projects freed from the constraints of permanent architecture, which "can often be non-traditional and even somewhat radical and able to accommodate non-conventional events and works" that promote cultural exchange. Lyn Rice, a partner at OpenOffice, an art and architecture collaborative in New York, believes that such projects have an immediacy and presence that particularly resonate in the built environment. He recalls architect Nasrine Seraji's temporary American Center in Paris that was installed in 1991 as having "an energy and the kind of excitement of a permanent structure at 80% completion." Made from commonplace materials such as plywood and polycarbonate sheeting, the raw, unfinished quality of the center was "unexpected and initiated interaction."

One of the most ambitious design programs is the Serpentine Gallery's Annual Architecture Commission. Designers are given the opportunity to produce a one-off pavilion to be situated adjacent to the gallery in Hyde Park, London. This project not only provides an additional exhibition and events space for the gallery, but also enables architects to experiment with geometries and materials. The resulting design can be used to promote their ideas and the experience inevitably informs their permanent projects. This summer, Brazilian architect Oscar Niemeyer with Cecil Balmond of Arup Europe developed an open-sided structure accessed by ramps with an indoor auditorium. The sloping structure appeared to unfold from the ground creating the impression that the building was an extension of the parkscape. Open daily from June to September and until late on evenings when free programs are offered (film screenings, lectures and other events) the pavilions create an interesting experiment in geometry and space rarely found in Hyde Park.

Projects that deliberately provoke exploration of public spaces can change perceptions, eliciting fresh thinking about familiar sites and contexts. One such project, Traffic, a 24-hour installation by New York-based artists/architects Diller + Scofidio performed in 1981, prompted reassessment of the habitual negotiations that often become seamlessly embedded in daily patterns of behavior and therefore overlooked but are essential to navigating public space. 2,500 orange traffic cones were placed in neat rows in New York's Columbus Circle forcing the public to find new routes through the space and to become aware of the prescribed urban plan of the street. Variable City: Fox Square, a performance and urban study, spearheaded by visual artist Julia Mandle and urban designer Ariel Krasnow, organized in fall 2003, altered pedestrian and traffic flow in an effort to "profoundly change the status quo." Dancers dressed in denim and traffic-cone-orange-colored wraptops created by Mandle, took control of Fox Square in Brooklyn, New York (an area slated

View of Serpentine Gallery's 2003 pavilion, Hyde Park, London, United Kingdom

RENDERING: OSCAR NIEMEYER

Left, top to bottom:

View of MoMA/P.S.1 Annual Young Architects Program, in the P.S.1 courtyard, Long Island City, Queens, New York, 2003

PHOTO: COURTESY MOMA/P.S.1

View of installation in the plaza in front of the Museum of Contemporary Art, Chicago, 2003

PHOTO: COURTESY OF MUSEUM OF CONTEMPORARY ART, CHICAGO

View of pavilion, Aarhus Theater Festival, Demark, 1996

PHOTO: ASYMPTOTE

View of temporary American Center, Paris

PHOTO: NASRINE SERAJI

View of Variable City: Fox Square performance, Brooklyn, New York

PHOTO: EMILY DRAZEN

for development) with unannounced performances choreographed by Mark Jarecke. The dancers either performed together on the central plaza or dispersed across the intersection to striking effect, interrupting the relentless hustle and bustle of people and vehicular traffic. The response from unsuspecting passersby was varied. Some asked questions, others were eager to read more about the project and took copies of the flyer available, while others seemed to ignore the dancers and strolled determinedly through the middle of a performance with or without realizing they were in fact part of the urban drama unraveling around them.

Eduardo López, a choreographer, has adopted this theme of rereading and understanding our environment. He encourages us, through dance, to "learn to look at a place in a new way, reinforcing social interaction and fostering tolerance." In July 2003 he directed the Days of Dance Festival, which took place in Barcelona at the Center for Contemporary Culture. Simultaneously staged in multiple sites around the city, the festival brought together thousands of residents and visitors, aimed at "opening a different vision of artistic and cultural heritage inherent to each city."

The Mexican artist Rafael Lozano-Hemmer also has a mission to "foster eccentric readings of the city" through projects that interrupt the "narratives of the urban realm," displacing people from their familiar environments and prompting them to develop their own "readings and subtitles." His aims are underscored by a concern that people no longer feel represented by cities, asserting that images that proliferate on billboards and hoardings signify a globalized and homogenous view of life as seen through the lens of corporations who employ strategic marketing tools to portray a specific message. "Cities are saturated with images and messages but they rarely show diversity and do not relate on an intimate level with the public," he explains. In his installations the public is the performer. "The challenge is to develop anti-monumental strategies for engaging the public; interventions that create platforms for people to both participate in and take over public space by amplifying them to an urban scale." Dividing his time between Madrid and Québec, Lozano-Hemmer develops electronic art works that range dramatically in scale. He has produced work for the Istanbul Biennial, the Ars Electronica in Austria and the Museo de Monterrey in Mexico. In November 2003, for the inauguration of the Yamaguchi Center for Arts and Media in Japan, Lozano-Hemmer produced Amodal Suspension, the largest interactive artwork in the world. Inviting people to send text messages over the Internet or by cell phone he then converted them into patterns of flashing lights in the sky, "turning the Japanese city of Yamaguchi into a giant communication switchboard." His most physically engaging project to date, Body Movies, which was staged in Schowburg Square, Rotterdam, the Netherlands, during the 2001 Cultural Capital of Europe events, and in Hauptplatz, Linz, Austria, and Williamson Square, Liverpool, United Kingdom in 2002. Lozano-Hemmer refers to the work, which features screens up to 75 feet in height and 200 feet in width, installed in well-trafficked areas of the city center as "Relational Architecture." Thousands of portraits, photographed on the streets of the cities where the project is to be shown, are projected onto the screens in succession but are over-exposed by the powerful light source shone onto them making them shadows. As people cross in front of the lights their silhouettes also appear in tandem with the preexisting portraits, up to 100-feet in height. As the images change, the public is encouraged to match their shadow with those featured on the screen. More than 60 people can take part at any one time enhancing the collective experience of being in public space. "My work does not push a message, but it does not exist without public participation," explains Lozano-Hemmer. "Because they are temporary they are not subsumed into the everyday patterns of life and therefore their presence invites surprising results as people begin to play intuitively with the shadows and control the space with their bodies."

British-born, Paris-based artist Lucy Orta's work has a similar social theme. Through predominantly proactive performances and sculptures she explores human interconnec-

Right top: View of Paris Plage, France

PHOTO: DIANA BALMORI

Right bottom: View of Body Movies, Hauptplatz, Linz, Austria, 2002

PHOTO: RAFAEL LOZANO-HEMMER

View of Delta Spirit by David Hammons, Art on the Beach, New York, 1985

PHOTO: LAWRENCE LESMAN
COURTESY OF CREATIVE TIME

Right top: View of 70 X 7 The Meal: Act V-VII Mexico City, Mexico, 2001

PHOTO: MATHIEU ROUSSEAUX

Right bottom: View of The Gates, Central Park, New York, 2005

PHOTO: WOLFGANG VOLZ
© CHRISTO, 2003

tivity. 70 X 7: The Meal, now in its 10th Act, brings people together "to meet, to talk and to share a moment of reflection." The Meal is for seven guests who in turn invite seven and symbolizes the biblical reference meaning "infinite." The idea was inspired by the work of Padre Rafael García Herreros who organized a series of banquets to raise money for a social development project in Bogotá. Reinterpreted by Lucy and her partner Jorge Orta, The Meal has been organized to foster communal interaction. In March 2003, the project transfigured: 70 x 7: Bowl of Rice for Peace, brought together 490 guests from around the world at the Paris headquarters of UNESCO for a "moment to pause, reflect and act for peace." Prior to this, the project focused specifically on bringing entire towns or communities together. In June 2002, 168 people, drawn from different socio-cultural groups and nationalities were invited to dine together on tables set out in a circle in Waltherplatz, Bolzano's central piazza in Italy. The year before, in Mexico City, 900 guests dined at three locations (including Couvent de la Mercedes, one of the city's oldest convents); in 2000, in Dieuze, in northeast France, 3,000 people, the entire population of the town, picnicked at a table that ran the length of the main high street. Orta asserts her mission by saying, "The city is not a décor; it is a vital space for interaction and a hub for social activity, a vector for exchange and an ever-changing scenario in which to intervene."

New York-based artists Christo and Jeanne-Claude dramatically intervene in the public realm to startling effect. Their most recent project The Gates, Central Park, New York has been on the boards since 1979. Originally rejected, the project was finally given the go-ahead in 2003 by New York City Mayor Michael R. Bloomberg on condition that holes are not dug in the ground, and that use of the park is not disturbed. Christo and Jeanne-Claude are known for their large-scale temporary art works in urban and rural spaces. Wrapped Reichstag Berlin 1971-95 was first conceived in 1971 but it took 25 years before the German government gave permission for it to be realized. In 1995, it was seen by five million people and has retained its power through documentation and memory long after it was removed. Other works, such as Surrounded Islands, Biscayne Bay, Miami, Florida 1980-83 are often only seen in person by a few but live on in books and films, revealing the magnitude of the work. Their work, which often takes years to come to fruition and enormous resources, is entirely self-funded, paid for through the sale of preparatory drawings, scale models, earlier works, and original lithographs. The process of achieving their vision is an important part of their work. Scheduled for February 2005, The Gates comprises 7,500 vinyl gates, 16 feet high, hung with saffron colored fabric. They will be placed 10 to 15 feet apart for 23 miles. This installation, along the edges of the pathways through Central Park, promises to be a spectacular saturation of color that will dramatically alter the nature of the urban parkscape.

In *Dialogues in Public Art* (MIT Press, 2000) Tom Finkelpearl laments the demise of Art on the Beach, an outdoor art event organized by Creative Time in the early 1980s, due to the "encroachment of the developer's bulldozers." Looking back, Finkelpearl writes, "I still think of the evening when I heard Sun Ra. I think of the modesty and originality of the architecture of Delta Spirit House, as well as the social and racial diversity of the crowd who had come to the concert." So begins his insightful volume on the role of public art in the development of a city, which he marks as vital in moving "toward sharing power rather than imposing solutions, toward healing wounds inflicted by the fragmentation and social integration of contemporary public space." Finkelpearl asserts the importance of temporary interventions in providing an armature for the public to rediscover their own environment and as stimulators of social engagement in public space. For designers and artists they provide an opportunity to test out their ideas, to perceive first hand the public response to their work and to bring the results of that research to bear on permanent work. Equally important, they raise awareness of the social implications of the urban environment and foster an essential dialogue between the public and the developer that can have a profound impact on the city.

The Gates (Project for Central Park, New York City) Central Park South, 5th Avenue, Columbus Circle, Central Park West, Cathedral PKWY, West 110th Street; 7500 Gates along 23 miles selected walkways

height 16'0" between each gate 12'0"

DESIGN OF/FOR/BY THE PUBLIC

Raymond W. Gastil and
Jonathan Cohen-Litant

The following initiatives—three recent North American competitions and four prominent sites in New York City—demonstrate, in very different ways, the relationship between design and public participation. From a long and clearly structured public consultation process that led to a four-stage international design competition in Toronto, to a simple, but effective, one-night event celebrating the recent opening of Southpoint in Roosevelt Island, all these projects reveal the importance that the public gives to having an impact on the use and design of what is, legally, their space. As any dialogue with visual representation involves political risk, these projects show that it is well worth taking.

NORTH AMERICAN COMPETITIONS

In North America, design competitions have had a history of stops and starts for public spaces, despite their strong beginnings such as the competition for New York's Central Park in 1858. Typically, memorials and monuments have been the most likely candidates for competitions, yet whether open or invited, or for a park, memorial, urban infrastructure, or even 16 acres in the country's third largest central business district, a competition is one of the most powerful techniques that a city has at its disposal to shape the future of its public life. The three competitions presented here offer a range of clients, geographies, programs, and intentions. Each of these examples encourages public participation at different stages of the design process—before, during, and/or after.

Model of Portland Aerial Tram competition winning entry

PHOTO: ANGELIL/GRAHAM/PFENINGER/SCHOLL

AERIAL TRAMWAY FOR PORTLAND, OREGON

The 2003 "North Macadam–Marquam Hill Aerial Tram International Design Competition" (Portland's first international design competition), sponsored by Portland Aerial Transportation, Inc. (PATI) and the City of Portland, invited four firms to present design ideas for how the tram would be architecturally inspiring and at the same time meet high aspirations for urban design and public spaces at its terminus points, on Marquam Hill and the North Macadam waterfront redevelopment area, for which the city (population 540,000) had adopted a renewal plan in 1999.

The competition was one-stage, and explicit that the purpose was not to arrive at a design proposal, but at the firm best suited to the job. To do this, the competition included public presentations by four invited teams led by: Angelil/Graham/Pfenninger/Scholl Architecture (AGPS); Guy Nordenson and Associates; SHoP (Sharples Holden Pasquarelli); and UN Studio.

In March 2003, AGPS were selected for their "clear understanding of the site's history and evolving possibilities, without losing sight of the technical problems to be solved." In November 2003, they presented their schematic design to the public during an "Open House." A citizen's advisory committee has been formed to provide public input to PATI, the city and the design team, which itself is expected to engage the community in the design process.

View of AGPS' Aerial Tram design, Portland, Oregon

RENDERING: ANGELIL/GRAHAM/PFENNINGER/SCHOLL

BEALE STREET LANDING
MEMPHIS, TENNESSEE

The "Shaping the New American Riverfront International Design Competition," sponsored by The Memphis Riverfront Development Corporation (RDC) in partnership with the City of Memphis, is planned to yield designs for a unique public space at the west end of Beale Street, linking the grid of the city to the riverfront and to Tom Lee Park to the south, with a dock that welcomes passenger boats from small pleasure craft to large river cruisers. A key site within the master plan developed by Cooper Robertson & Partners in 2001, it has the twenty-five-foot bluff on the east, where downtown sits, and the volatile Mississippi River on the west. To the north, "the cobblestones" are an early 19th-century legacy of a once-active harbor wharf, now used as a parking lot.

This international two-stage design competition, the first of its kind for this city of 600,000 began in 2003. Five finalist teams were selected from 171 submissions to visit the site during the summer, and develop their designs for the second stage of the competition. Throughout this period, the public were encouraged to comment on the designs and share ideas for the site through a comprehensive and informative web site that was developed as an interactive tool.

The winning design, selected in October 2003, referred to as "River Outlook," by RTN Architects of Buenos Aires, Argentina, consists of a series of level, landscaped islands formed in the ramped slope of the river's edge creating spaces for casual and formal use. These "islets" or outlooks, connected by pedestrian bridges, are buttressed to withstand the forces of the river, as well as reveal the stages of the Mississippi River, which, in a typical year, vary as much as fifty feet.

View of RTN Architects' proposal for the Memphis riverfront, Memphis, Tennessee

MODEL:RTN ARCHITECTS

TORONTO'S LAKEFRONT

The Harbourfront Parks and Open Space Design Competition, sponsored by the City of Toronto and directed by the city's Economic Development, Culture, and Tourism Department, asked for a design approach for the fifteen acres of public space parklands that remain to be completed in the 40-acre waterfront district, which was designated and began development a decade ago. Toronto, which undertook an in-depth study of its waterfront as part of a metropolitan region and larger ecology in the early 1990s, is now focusing on realizing the promise of a downtown lakefront that is engaging enough to overcome the challenge of being, like many North American urban waterfronts, cut off from the central business district by a major highway.

Public participation here has been a critical building block for the eventual completion of this unique urban park system. The City engaged residents, user groups, and other key stakeholders in a public dialogue in 2002 to assist in developing a vision for the parks and open space system.

The first phase of the competition, a call for expressions of interest, was followed by a second stage in which finalists, after participating in a collaborative workshop, then proceeded to work individually on conceptual designs. The collaborative process was an unusual one for a design competition, which put competitors together to develop a collective vision. The multidisciplinary teams, led by Phillips Farevaag Smallenberg, Gustafson Guthrie Nichol Ltd, and Janet Rosenberg Associates (HTO), reflect the complexity of envisioning successful public space at this scale

The jury selected the winning design created by HTO, and in June 2003 it was approved. The design is based on six elements or layers: ground planes, water, islands, expressive horticulture, lighting and beach furniture.

Bird's eye view of HTO's design for the Harbourfront, Toronto, Canada

RENDERING: HTO

NEW IN NEW YORK

FROM LANDSCAPE TO "LIFESCAPE,"
FRESH KILLS, STATEN ISLAND

Top: Aerial view of Field Operations' design proposal for Fresh Kills, Staten Island, New York

IMAGE: FIELD OPERATIONS

In response to the planned closing of New York's largest "engineered" landscape (at almost three times the size of Central Park), the Fresh Kills landfill on Staten Island, the city held a two-stage, international design competition to develop a master plan and design vision for the site's future. The New York City Department of City Planning ran the project with the assistance of the Departments of Sanitation, Parks and Recreation, and Cultural Affairs, and the Municipal Art Society, and with early support from the National Endowment for the Arts. It called for the expertise of teams of professionals in design, engineering, ecology, art, and planning. This was a bold venture, given the technical and political complexities of the site and its role in the city.

More than fifty interdisciplinary teams responded. Six were chosen to develop their schemes. After the last barge floated over to unload its waste in March 2001, no one imagined that six months later the landfill would reopen to take the wreckage from the World Trade Center attacks. The finalists were asked to recognize this in some way as part of their schemes, and these memorials were integrated into the presentations in December 2001.

In December, "LIFESCAPE," a proposal led by Field Operations proved the most compelling. The project re-imagined Staten Island as the exemplar of a contemporary, future-looking metropolis, in which leisure and natural systems were highly valued and integral to life. In their vision, Fresh Kills was connected to networks of greenways and waterways that would allow the former "dump" to become the generator of a new identity for the fifth borough. The envisioned phasing includes recreation areas adjacent to the surrounding neighborhoods of Travis and Arden Heights and a reserve of forests and wetlands.

Following Mayor Bloomberg's announcement in September 2003, Field Operations began work on a conceptual design and public outreach on the Fresh Kills End Use Master Plan. A New York Department of City Planning website has been developed to provide public information and gather community input.

2012 AND BEYOND FOR FLUSHING MEADOWS, QUEENS, NEW YORK

New York's planning for the Olympics in 2012 has made New Yorkers see the city and its parks in a new way, and may already have a positive legacy, with or without winning the games in 2005.

In 2001, NYC2012 commissioned Weiss/Manfredi Architects to design how the games' rowing events could be held in Flushing Meadows-Corona Park, the site of the 1939 and the 1964 worlds fairs, close to the rapidly evolving community of Flushing, Queens. The first goal was simply to prove that it could be done—that there was space for flat-water and white-water courses and for the media and spectators who would be watching them, a goal that expanded into more complex design development as New York was chosen in fall 2002 to be the U.S. candidate for the games. The architects, who have addressed the relationship of infrastructure to natural systems and contemporary recreation in projects nationwide, worked with a team of landscape architects and ecology experts, engineers, and a rowing consultant to demonstrate how a new kind of park could both meet the intense temporary needs of the Olympics and also leave a valuable ecological and recreational legacy for the neighborhood and the city.

The marshland site, divided and isolated by highways, is re-envisioned as having three main components. The flat-water course, which reconnects two lakes to meet the 2000-meter course requirement, is lined by boathouses, docks, and spectator seating, and there's a new bridge over to replace the roadway that ran between the formerly divided lakes. The whitewater course, directly east of the iconic 1964 Unisphere, takes the former circular reflecting pool and reconfigures it as a spiral with the 20-foot drop needed for the course. The interior face of the huge spiral, spun out of the circle, has seating for 15,000, while the berms at its periphery overlook soccer fields. The ecological infrastructure, as the designers describe it, "includes a preprogramming of the existing infrastructure with an ecological imperative." The resulting design links the parts of the park divided by highway with elevated boardwalks, creating a new wetland terrain that captures storm water, and supports new plant life as well as bird and animal habitats.

View of model of NYC2012 proposal, Flushing Meadows-Corona Park, Queens, New York

PHOTO: WEISS/MANFREDI ARCHITECTS

Top: View of Weiss/ Manfredi's NYC2012 proposal, Flushing Meadows-Corona Park, Queens, New York

PHOTO: WEISS/MANFREDI ARCHITECTS

BROOKLYN BRIDGE PARK,
BROOKLYN, NEW YORK

In spring 2002, New York State's Governor and NYC's Mayor announced plans for the Brooklyn Bridge Park, financed by New York State through the Port Authority of New York and New Jersey, and by the City. Years of work had led to this announcement, including the illustrative master plan or "framework" for the 67-acre site released in September 2000, which incorporated the expertise and energies of thousands of community residents and the long-active Brooklyn Bridge Park Coalition, who participated in scores if not hundreds of meetings, and the professional skills of dozens of consultants, including those who led the 2000 design/planning effort led by the Downtown Brooklyn Waterfront Local Development Corporation (DBWLDC). The DBWLDC enlisted a team to prepare the master plan that included HR&A Associates, Ken Greenberg, Raymond Gindroz, and Michael Van Valkenburgh Associates. The 2002 announcement marked the formation of the Brooklyn Bridge Park Development Corporation (BBPDC), a subsidiary of New York State's Empire State Development Corporation, which now leads the effort to realize the park.

The piers 1-5 portion of this waterfront, which includes huge industrial pier-sheds overlooking the mouth of the East River, sits below Brooklyn Heights and to the west of the stacked layers of the Brooklyn-Queens Expressway. The overall site extends from Atlantic Avenue on the south of the piers up to the base of the Brooklyn Bridge, past the Empire Stores warehouses, and on to Jay Street north of Manhattan Bridge. The proposal calls for mostly open space, from soccer fields to fishing piers, and plazas, as well as revenue-producing retail and hotel and conference proposals.

In April 2003, the BBPDC completed the park's Concept Plan, revising and refining the proposals from the illustrative master plan. In the same month, the BBPDC called for proposals from eight design teams, including landscape architecture and architecture firms, as well as engineers, economic consultants, sustainability experts, and artists.

The park has faced innumerable challenges: divided community attitudes, multiple ownerships, debates over private enterprises on public land, local fears of citywide use. The BBPDC invited a remarkable range of designers, and in June 2003 it has selected a new design team headed by Michael Van Valkenburgh Associates, including Sol Lewitt, Gensler, James Carpenter and others. During the next year, MVVA will be concentrating on preparing a Master Site Development Plan for the Park.

Illustrative Master Plan,
Brooklyn Bridge Park, New York,
September 2000

DRAWING: MICHAEL VAN VALKENBURGH ASSOCIATES

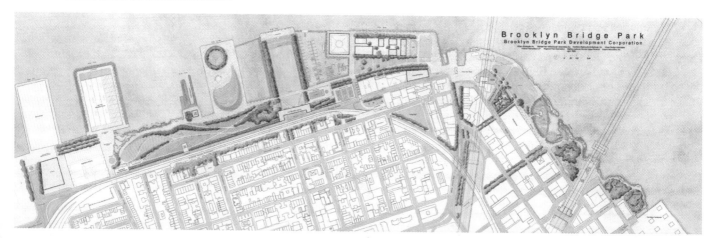

View of Southpoint, Roosevelt Island, New York

PHOTO: JONATHAN COHEN-LITANT

SOUTHPOINT,
ROOSEVELT ISLAND, NEW YORK

The southern tip of Roosevelt Island has been the subject of design and development proposals for decades. Southpoint is about ten acres, pointing out into the East River at the southern tip of the almost two-mile-long island. At the center of the site is the landmarked ruin of the Smallpox Hospital designed by James Renwick in 1856, while the southern end is spectacularly sited at the center of the East River, between the rising towers of Queens West on the left bank and the United Nations on the right. Southpoint was off-limits to visitors from 1982 until this spring, except for an annual 4th of July firework display. Not that it suffered from a dearth of ideas: in 1974 Louis Kahn designed a memorial to Franklin Delano Roosevelt, only a year after the island was named in his honor, and later Santiago Calatrava designed a restaurant, and most recently a twin-tower Marriott Hotel and conference center were proposed.

Now it has a different idea—a park with few frills but a great site and an eager public. The Roosevelt Island Operating Corporation (RIOC), a New York State public authority, opened the park in April 2003. Ultimately, the site will be more fully improved, but it is important to note that even in fiscally challenging times for state and municipal governments, public parkland can be brought into the public realm.

In August 2003, on a Saturday evening, Van Alen Institute, in partnership with Rooftop Films, the Roosevelt Island Historical Society, and RIOC, hosted a free outdoor screening (OPEN views: Films on the City) in celebration of the recent opening of Southpoint. More than a 1000 New Yorkers poured in, demonstrating their appetite for new, exceptional public spaces.

INTERNATIONAL PERSPECTIVES ON PUBLIC SPACE

The rethinking of the design of public spaces is an international phenomenon. The following commentaries reflect the insights of architects, planners, critics, and others from Barcelona, Bogotá, Chicago, Johannesburg, and London. The situations and responses are diverse yet these commentaries illustrate the critical role of public spaces (both those included in the *OPEN* exhibition and beyond) in defining 21st-century cities.

IN FAVOR OF PUBLIC SPACE

Josep Ramoneda is director of the Center of Contemporary Culture, Barcelona (CCCB)

The question of public space is accompanied–maybe motivated–by concern over the state of democracy. This is a constant. It is hardly surprising, given that the city, democracy, politics, and philosophy appeared together in ancient Greece. They were the fruit of the irruption of the dissociate laws of logos and the result of society going beyond the organic nature of pre-urban life, bestowing each and every person a destiny that was marked by irrefutable nature. Unity is not the object of the city because the city is pluralism, as Aristotle tells us.

The symbolic place in which city, democracy, and politics are to be found is public space. Each time the bells toll for democracy (and we are now at a time when the future of democracy looks grim), we think about the state of public space and vice versa. Growing concern with public space–in spite of the ideological pressure against anything that might represent places for relating, for community, for complicity–is an expression of concern about the state of democracy and for the future of politics in a "liquid modernity" (Zygmunt Bauman) or a "modernity without modernism" (Jonathan Friedman). I do not wish to engage in the snobbery of the discourse that pronounces that the city is dead, that democracy is dead and public space is dead. This may be some kind of sensationalist ploy, which guarantees success in a society that is all show, but it is too trite to be taken seriously. Once the death of sense has been pronounced–which is what all this necrological passion amounts to–what remains? Maybe the world makes no sense, but sense is necessary for life. This is why we are ceaselessly creating and re-creating new sense. It is the task –Sisyphean, perhaps–of the species. It is true that nothing is eternal. However, it is also true that humanity tends to produce a metamorphosis of sense and institutions rather than opting for definitive abolition and radical substitutions. The old almost always appears in the new–even where the rupture appears to be irreversible, as with Soviet Russia for example–and new generations frequently do nothing more than to bring into existence what the previous generation has already thought.

The symbolic weight of public space is very great. Public space is the place for public use of reason in opposition to private use of reason, according to Kant's distinction. Public use of reason entails the unlimited freedom to call upon reason itself and to speak in its name. Private use is domestic and is often subject to regulation. However, this distinction is suffused with Enlightenment optimism and a faith in reason that is very rarely found in these times.

Public space marks the limits of the idea of the city. Where it does not exist, one may speak of urbanization but not really of the city. It is therefore encouraging to see, if we bear in mind the link between the city and democracy, how people can form public spaces out of nothing, even in the most disjointed megalopolis. At the same time, the contempt shown for public space by some of the conservative parties in Europe–they can tell us all about it in Madrid–is a good reflection of the idea of democracy held by those who govern us. Nowadays, it is the right that breaks the limits, that believes that anything is possible. And there are times when one wonders whether there is a strategically motivated will to destroy the city.

This is an abridged version of the article published in El País on July 29, 2003, which was written following the "(In)Visible Cities: Spaces of Risk, Spaces of Citizenship," conference organized by the Center of Contemporary Culture, Barcelona in July 2003

THE PEDESTRIAN IN THE NEW THIRD WORLD CITY

Enrique Peñalosa is the former Mayor of Bogotá, Colombia, and a Visiting Scholar at The Center for Latin American and Caribbean Studies (CLACS), New York University

The rethought third world city has a few basic characteristics: It is surrounded by a large expanse of publicly owned land both for parks and for lower income high quality housing, so as to avoid forcing the poor into slums. It is dense, yet without high-rises, so as to permit good low-cost public transport and in order to have significant amounts of people in public spaces. It has abundant parks, plazas and sport facilities. It is crisscrossed by an important network of large pedestrian roads that are the city's vital axis. Everywhere it has large tree-lined sidewalks, continuous at the same level regardless of garage entrances and minor street crossings. Automobile use except for taxis is not allowed during peak morning and afternoon hours; citizens use public transport or bicycles during those times. It has bicycle ways physically isolated from motor-vehicle traffic in all streets. The measure of success is how good the city is for children, the aged, and the handicapped.

We humans are pedestrians. We need to walk, not in order to survive, but to be happy. A bird can survive inside a cage and even reproduce itself inside that small space. Yet one suspects the bird would be happier in a cage the size of an auditorium and better still flying free. Just as the bird, we can survive inside an apartment all our life, but we are of course happier if we can go out and walk. And we feel better if there is a sidewalk, better still if it is a 10-meter wide sidewalk than one that is 3-meters, and even better if it is an exclusively pedestrian street, free from the noise and threat of motor vehicles next to it. This is not something that can be proven mathematically.

Over the last 80 years we have been making cities much more for cars' mobility than for children's happiness. In the new city pedestrians and bicyclists should be given as much importance as motor vehicles; even more so in developing country cities, where most homes don't own cars. Traditionally in Europe, pedestrian networks are located in historic centers. But we can create magnificent pedestrian roads in growth areas around our cities and through the poorest, recently informal neighborhoods.

Someone may question why public pedestrian space is important at all in societies with so much poverty related problems. In fact it may be more important there than in advanced countries. Reduced to very small living spaces, the lower income urban citizens in a developing country have public space as their only leisure alternative. It is indeed during leisure times that income differences are felt more acutely. Higher income citizens have many alternatives to public space: i.e. ample houses and gardens, cars for traveling to the countryside, country houses, clubs and restaurants. Lower income children's only leisure time alternative to television is public pedestrian space.

We recovered and built hundreds of sidewalks and a 15-meter-wide, 17-kilometer-long pedestrian promenade through some of the city's poorest neighborhoods and through empty lots soon to be urbanized. This is a new concept of a pedestrian street. Europeans have been turning their historic city centers into pedestrian only areas. But we believed we could best incorporate major pedestrian roads in new developments and future city plans.

From having an extremely negative attitude towards itself, Bogotá has become a city with a sense of belonging and confidence in a better future thanks to the implementation of a different city model. It stems from successful experiences elsewhere, an appraisal of our differences and aspirations and a realistic look at our possibilities. Our proposed model is neither technologically sophisticated, nor economically demanding. It requires, however, political decisions aimed at truly making public good prevail.

This text is abbreviated and adapted from "Rethinking Third World Cities' Transport" (International Union of Public Transport, UITP, Madrid, 2003.)

PUBLIC SPACE?
IN JOHANNESBURG?

Henning Rasmuss is director of Paragon Architects (Pty.) Ltd., Johannesburg with Anthony Orelowitz. In 2003, he curated the "Johannesburg Metropolis" exhibition at the Sao Paulo Biennale, Brazil

The life of cities occurs in public space. People activate public space in order to live the choices city life offers, and to project their identity and their desires into and onto a landscape that is a given and a constant.

Johannesburg is defined by a number of qualities, one of these being its ability and willingness to rush headlong into the future. At only 117 years of age, it is too young to be precious about itself, or about where it is going. Its psyche, shaped by its history of gold, is centered on exploitation and convenient reinvention.

It is hardly a city known for the quality of its public spaces: it has simply not been designed around them. It has always been a city of corporate showmanship, and even its civic architecture is at best part of a street, hardly ever part of a popular urban space. Beyond the city and its monuments lie vast stretches of intensely private suburbs with free-standing houses; be they villas of the rich or the township housing of the poor. In an exploitative and private city such as Johannesburg, what is public space?

Ten years into a democratic order, we are still struggling to understand the impact of being citizens of one nation, let alone being equal citizens of one city. If public space has to absorb the everyday and functional, but more importantly the symbolic needs of city life, what does our relationship to public space say about us as a society?

Ten years ago, Johannesburg was released into a chaos of freedom. With the end of apartheid's spatial ordering system, the city became, more than ever, a landscape to be exploited by all. In the power vacuum between political orders, management of the city deteriorated. The resulting free space allowed mercenary operators to occupy and colonize the few public spaces the city had: taxi ranks and shopping centers replaced open space, and we lost the safety of the streets. Security paranoia caused walls to rise and houses to turn in on themselves.

Are there projects which challenge this dominant trend? I believe they are only just beginning to be formed. And they will have to reverse a way of life we have come to accept all too readily.

Perhaps we have realized one thing: in order for public space to exist and to add to real quality of life, public buildings need to support it. Good public buildings which absorb real needs. Here, our new market structures and taxi ranks have allowed our streets and pavements to work for ordinary citizens once more.

Where public space becomes a free-for-all, its usefulness declines. For a while, we believed that freedom in itself was worthy of expression in the city. We celebrated the new structures, textures, vibrancy, visual chaos, and pure efficiency and inventiveness of the takeover of public space in the newfound freedom of our cities. But we forgot that successful public space depends on a social contract between city and individual.

Coming from a culture of separation and discrimination in space, we have learnt our lessons fast as our young city changed in true Johannesburg style. We have gone from a discriminatory city to a chaotic city that began to fail at every level. Now we are heading in the right direction, I believe, and new projects such as the Kliptown Renewal Project show the way.

Why? Because this project has a genuine aim at a better life for all users of the city. This project represents a negotiated solution to the conflicting claims on land and its uses. This is a solution aimed at empowering ordinary people to be proud and active players in their life and in the life of the community. This project provides genuinely useful spaces. This project carries with it programmes of learning and skills transfer. Here, people benefit not from spaces, but from being involved in the process of creation of spaces.

Here is an architecturally ambitious project that does simple things with limited means. They show how we can, in our own hurried way, take some of the best lessons from greater and more accomplished cities, and apply them to the benefit of ordinary people. And celebrate not consensus, but difference acted out with respect for others. That is a powerful driver for successful Public Space.

NOTES ON PUBLIC SPACE

Rowan Moore is director of the Architecture Foundation in London, and architecture critic of the *London Evening Standard*

As a journalist, writing for the *London Evening Standard*, I find that any article that takes "public space" as its subject is particularly laborious to write and, to judge by the tepid responses of editors and readers, to read. (And, yes, this too is an article about public space, but as it is a short one I would be grateful for your perseverance in getting to the end.)

This laboriousness is a sure sign that that there is something not quite right about the phrase "public space," that is so often wheeled out, dutifully but rarely with pleasure or relish. It is an insubstantial concept, compared with more graspable words like "street," "tower," "bridge" or "house." It is also one of those phrases used by architects and related professionals, but rarely anyone else. No one says "I am going to the public space this afternoon." Yet we all know individual examples of public spaces that are highly graspable, and inspire pleasure and relish.

The problem seems to be that the phrase suppresses the complexities, diversity and gradations of the things it describes. Tiffany Jenkins, of the Institute of Ideas in London, observes that the people who talk most about public space are often those who feel most insecure about its use and occupation: they talk about it as something for someone other than themselves, as a thing for "the general public," to use another dodgy term. The conventional descriptions of public space, by architects and politicians, refer to something generic and non-specific, and therefore boring. Under these descriptions the success of spaces is always calibrated by the numbers of people occupying it, rather than any more subtle consideration of the emotions and perceptions they permit.

So it's worth questioning some of the common assumptions about "public space":

Firstly there is no such thing as public space, just public spaces. Equally, there is no such thing as "the general public," just many publics. Places that work well belong to some people more than others, both legally and emotionally. Places that try to belong to everyone belong to no one. Successful places also have a purpose or purposes, as Jane Jacobs observed. Constructive emptiness, or places to reflect, can be one such purpose.

From this it follows that the definition of territories, often seen as suspect, is both inevitable and desirable: what matters is the way the boundaries and overlaps of these territories is negotiated. Contemporary liberal piety holds that suburban gated communities are bad, but that the Parisian apartment block is good, yet both consist of forty or so dwellings with a secure enclosure, and a monitored entrance. The difference is not in the fact of enclosure, but in the way it is done.

Secondly, there is no absolute distinction between public and private spaces, or a smooth scale from one state to the other. Rather there are inversions and paradoxes. Most people, for example, are more likely to experience a social situation involving six or more people in their home or workplace than in public places, where they will typically be alone or interacting with one or two others.

Almost all the spaces of a city are in fact impure. The restaurant, the shop, the theatre, the subway train, the hospital, the office—the places where people spend their lives —are hybrids of public and private.

Thirdly, the form of public spaces should not be confused with their content. The Djemaa El-Fna in Marrakesh, one of the most vigorous public places in the world, is virtually shapeless and devoid of architectural character, while places that take the official geometric shapes of public space, such as squares and circles, often fail.

These observations make the understanding of public spaces more complex, but they could also make life easier for those who try to shape them. They suggest that architects don't have to try so hard, or take on so much responsibility for the success of public space. Public life takes place of its own accord, and finds its own spaces. The principal task of architects is often to avoid getting in the way.

OUT-TAKE FROM CHICAGO

Ned Cramer is curator of
the Chicago Architecture
Foundation

On February 16, 2003, Chicago Mayor Richard M. Daley made a proclamation from the front page of the local *Sun-Times*: "No More Ugly Buildings." This just one year after the University of Illinois Chicago School of Architecture staged the "Chicago is History" conference, a wake of sorts where Daniel Libeskind and other luminaries bemoaned the loss of "innovation and experimentation" in Chicago architecture. Everyone has their own definition of "ugly," and while the *Sun-Times* article neglected to elaborate on Daley's, the most prominent public project of his 14-year administration, Millennium Park, may demonstrate what the mayor doesn't mean by "ugly." Progressives should be pleased; one could even argue that the park—along with a number of coincident new buildings in town by architects such as Helmut Jahn, Rem Koolhaas, and Wood + Zapata—marks a turn-around for architecture in Chicago.

Millennium Park, which is scheduled to open in 2004, features an undulated band shell and pedestrian bridge by Frank Gehry of Los Angeles, an asymmetric perennial garden by Seattle landscape architect Kathryn Gustafson, a pair of glass-block fountains outfitted for video projections by Spanish artist Jaume Plensa, and a 100-ton stainless-steel sculpture by Anglo-Indian artist Anish Kapoor that resembles an extra-large Elsa Peretti bean pendant from Tiffany. All this innovation and experimentation occurs within a beaux-arts master plan by the office of Skidmore, Owings & Merrill, replete with allées, parterres, and balustrades. An architect trained in the modernist tradition—a graduate of the University of Illinois Chicago, for instance, or of the Illinois Institute of Technology—might argue that making a new park, with innovative art and architecture, calls for a new and innovative master plan. In less prejudiced eyes, however, there is a perfectly good reason for the beaux-arts plan: It basically replicates the 1920s layout of Grant Park, of which Millennium Park is a part, and Grant Park emulates the 17th-century gardens of André LeNôtre at Versailles and the Tuileries, in keeping with architect Daniel Burnham's late-19th-century vision of Chicago as "Paris on the Prairie."

The debate between architectural progressives and conservatives has been going on for over a century in Chicago; it's practically a tradition in and of itself: When Burnham invited beaux-arts architects from the East Coast to design the 1893 World's Columbian Exposition in Chicago, Louis Sullivan complained that the decision "set back architecture fifty years." At Millennium Park, outsiders provided the innovative, experimental solution, as though native talent couldn't be trusted to do the job well. Millennium Park's organizers went with a safer variety of innovator, one proven elsewhere, as though there could be such a thing as innovation without risk. Local architects did get their fair share of work at Millennium Park, but they hardly got the opportunity to experiment: SOM got to redraw the 1920s master plan, and OWP&P got to rebuild a curved Doric colonnade from the same period, at four-fifths scale; Krueck + Sexton served as associates to Jaume Plensa; and Tom Beeby received the commission to design the Music and Dance Theater, buried underground, at the foot of Gehry's band shell.

Well after the other commissions at Millennium Park had been handed out, one of Chicago's most forward thinking architects, Doug Garofalo, was asked to design the area around Kapoor's sculpture. All early signs indicate that Garofalo will enjoy considerable creative license. There are no guarantees that his scheme will be built, but the mere fact of the commission can be taken as a promising sign that not only has Chicago once again become a safe place for architectural innovation and experimentation, but that perhaps Chicago architects soon will be given the chance to do the innovating and experimenting themselves.

Project Credits: The Plaza Unbound

OSLO NATIONAL OPERA HOUSE
OSLO, NORWAY

ARCHITECT	Snøhetta
CLIENT	STATSBYGG
DESIGN TEAM	Craig Dykers (Principal)
	Tarald Lundevall (Principal)
	Kjetil Traedal Thorsen (Principal)
	Martin Dietrichson
	Ibrahim El Hayawan
	Chandani Ratnawira
	Harriet Rikheim
	Marianne Saetre
CONSULTANTS	Ragnhild Momrak, MNLA (Landscape Architects)
	Inger Buresund (Director, Black Box Theatre)
	Axel Helstenius (Author)
	Henrik Helstenius (Composer)
	Peder Istad (Artist)
	Jorunn Sannes (Artist)
	Theatre Projects Consultants, Ltd.
	David Staples
	Mark Stroomer

FEDERATION SQUARE
MELBOURNE, AUSTRALIA

ARCHITECT	Lab Architecture Studio with Bates Smart
CLIENT	State Government of Victoria and City of Melbourne
DESIGN TEAM	Donald L. Bates (Principal)
	Peter Davidson (Principal)
	Tony Allen (Project Manager)
	Tim Hill
	James Murray
	Attilio Terragni
	Dylan Ingleton
	Bates Smart
CONSULTANTS	Bonacci Group (Structural Engineer)
	Karres en Brands (Landscape Architect)
	Hyder Consulting (Civil/Structural Engineer)
	Connell Wagner (Civil Engineer)
	Atelier One (Structural/Façade Engineer)
	Atelier Ten (Environmental Engineer)
	Marshall Day Acoustics (Acoustical Engineer)

CITY HALL,
LONDON, UNITED KINGDOM

ARCHITECT	Foster and Partners
CLIENT	More London Development Ltd.
DESIGN TEAM	Norman Foster (Principal)
	Ken Shuttleworth
	Andy Bow
	Stefan Behling
	Sean Affleck
	Richard Hyams
	Max Neal
CONSULTANTS	Arup
	Sir Anthony Caro
	Davis Langdon & Everest
	Claude R Engle Lighting
	Monberg & Thorsen/McAlpine
	Malcolm Reading & Associates

PONTE PARODI
GENOA, ITALY

ARCHITECT	UN Studio
CLIENT	Porto Antico Spa, Genoa, Italy
DESIGN TEAM	Caroline Bos (Principal)
	Ben Van Berkel (Principal)
	Tobias Wallisser
	Harm Wassink

Project Credits: Information in Place

INSTITUTE OF CONTEMPORARY ART
BOSTON, MASSACHUSETTS

ARCHITECT	Diller + Scofidio
CLIENT	Boston Institute of Contemporary Art
DESIGN TEAM	Elizabeth Diller (Principal)
	Ricardo Scofidio (Principal)
	Charles Renfro (Project Leader)
	Deane Simpson
	Eric Howeler
	Flavio Stigliano
	Jeff Atwood
	Janette Kim
	Tim Kreidel
	Jesse Saylor
	Gaspar Libendinsky
	Marten Wessel
CONSULTANTS	Ove Arup NY (Structural Engineer)
	Jaffe Holden Acoustics (Acoustics)
	Fisher Dachs Associates (Theater Consultant)
ASSOC. ARCHITECT	Perry Dean Rogers and Partners
CONTRACTOR	Macomber (Construction Manager)

FOURTH GRACE
LIVERPOOL, UNITED KINGDOM

ARCHITECT	Alsop Architects
CLIENT	Liverpool Vision/ North West Regional Development Corporation + Museums + Galleries on Merseyside
DESIGN TEAM	Will Alsop (Principal)
	Christophe Egret (Project Architect)
	Andy Lebisch
	James Hampton
	Thomas Wingate
CONSULTANTS	David West (Master planner)
	Arup (Design Consultation/Engineer)
	Countryside Properties (Program Manager)
	Neptune Developments Ltd. (Program Manager)

CHUNGMURO INTERMEDIA PLAYGROUND
SEOUL, KOREA

ARCHITECT	Minsuk Cho, James Slade and Kwang-Soo Kim (Cho Slade Architecture + team BAHN)
CLIENT	The Association of Korean Independent Film & Video commissioned by Seoul City Cultural Affairs Bureau
DESIGN TEAM	Minsuk Cho (Principal)
	James Slade (Principal)
	Kwang-Soo Kim (Principal)
	Jae-hyuk Huh
	Ju-en Yi
	Yi-jung Park
	Chul-whan Yi
	Hyo-suk Whang
	Francisco Pardo
	Ilya Korolev
CONSULTANTS	Jae Sang Jung (Engineering)
	Jip Hyun Jeon (Graphic Design)
	Kang Hyuk Lee (Materials)
	Yong Woo Kuwon (Cost Evaluation)
	Donghyo Intec. (Contracting)

ONE-NORTH SINGAPORE SCIENCE HUB
SINGAPORE

ARCHITECT	Zaha Hadid Architects
CLIENT	Science Hub Development Group (SHDG)
	Jurong Town Corporation (JTC)
DESIGN TEAM	Zaha M. Hadid (Principal)
	Markus Dochantshi (Project Manager)
	Silvia Forlati
	David Gerber
	Gunther Koppelhuber
	Dillon Linn
	David Mah
	Rodrigo O'Mally
	Kim Thornton
CONSULTANTS	Lawrence Barth, London (Urban Strategy)
	MVA, Singapore (Transport)
	ARUP, London (Infrastructure)
	JTC Consultants Private Limited (JCPL), Singapore (Infrastructure Audit)
	Cicada Private Limited, Singapore (Landscape Architecture)
	Lighting Planners Associates Inc. (LPA), Tokyo (Lighting)
	B consultants, London (Planning)

Project Credits: Opening the City

POPLAR STREET
MACON, GEORGIA

LANDSCAPE ARCHITECT	Hood Design
CLIENT	Macon-Bibb County Road Improvement Program
DESIGN TEAM	Walter Hood (Principal)
	Grace Lee (Project Landscape Architect)
CONSULTANTS	Dan Euser Water Architecture, Inc.
LANDSCAPE ARCHITECTS	Jelks McLees Boggs

ALAMEDA EL PORVENIR
BOGOTÁ, COLOMBIA

ARCHITECT	MGP Arquitectura y Urbanismo (MGP Architecture and Urbanism)
CLIENT	Office of the Mayor of Bogotá
	Enrique Peñalosa Londoño (Mayor 1997-2001)
	Instituto de Desarrollo Urbano (Urban Development Institute)
DESIGN TEAM	Felipe González-Pacheco Mejía (Principal)
	Juan Ignacio Muñoz Tamayo (Principal)
	Collaborators:
	Álvaro Bohórquez Rivero
	Sergio García Casas
	Francina Domínguez Dueñas
	José Lisímaco Cohecha Mesa
	Luis Antonio Fonseca
	Urban Design Institute:
	Andrés Camargo Ardila
	Alicia Naranjo Uribe
	Professional Public Space Studio
	Lorenzo Castro Jaramillo

FAVELA-BAIRRO PROJECT
RIO DE JANEIRO, BRAZIL

ARCHITECT	Jorge Mario Jáuregui Architects
CLIENT	Town Hall of the Rio de Janeiro City (Prefeitura Municipal do Rio de Janeiro- secretaria municipal de habitção)
DESIGN TEAM	Jorge Mario Jáuregui (Principal)
	Alexandre Costa
	Eduardo Trelles
	Eduardo de Carolis
	Robson Saramago
	Fábio Amaral
	Gabriel Leandro Jáuregui
CONSULTANTS	Hamilton Case (Landscape Architect)
	Fabio Amaral (Geographer)
	Diana Mariscal (Psychoanalyst)
	Pedro Aleixo (Land Tenure, Engineer)
	Pedro Cunca Bocayuva (Sociologist)
	Ivair Coelho Lisboa (Philosopher)
	Eduardo De Carolis (Infrastructure, Engineer)
CONTRACTOR	Presitec engenharia, ltda.
ENGINEER	Eduardo de Carolis
	Robson Saramago

ARTSCAPE, A13
LONDON, UNITED KINGDOM

ARCHITECT	de Paor Architects
CLIENT	London Borough of Barking and Dagenham
DESIGN TEAM	Tom de Paor (Principal)
	Jeremy Grint (Head of Regeneration)
	Tracy McNulty (Head of Arts)
	Peter Watson, LBBD (Project Manager)
	A. Cochrane
	T. Maher
	K. Smith
CONSULTANTS	Geoff Wood (P.ARTS)
	J. Poncelet
	London Borough of Barking and Dagenham (Civil Engineer)

Project Credits: New Meeting Grounds

ISLAND IN THE MUR
GRAZ, AUSTRIA

ARCHITECT	Acconci Studio
CLIENT	Graz 2003 – Cultural Capital of Europe OrganisationsGmbH
DESIGN TEAM	Vito Acconci (Principal) Kurt Kratzer (Project Manager) Stephen Roe Peter Dorsey Thomas Siegl Gia Wolff Nan Wulffin Laura Charlton Sergio Prego
CONSULTANTS	Robert Punkenhofer/Art & Idea (Concept and Curatorial Development)
ASSOC. ARCHITECT	Purpur.cc Planconsult Austria
STRUCTURAL ENGINEERS	Zenkner and Handl
CONTRACTOR	SFL Playground Contractor: Corocord

MORI ART MUSEUM
ROPPONGI HILLS, TOKYO, JAPAN

ARCHITECT	Gluckman Mayner Architects
CLIENT	Mori Building Company, Limited
DESIGN TEAM	Richard Gluckman (Principal) David Mayner (Principal) Sam Brown (Project Manager) Taro Narahara Jasmit Rangr Kaori Sato
CONSULTANTS	Kohn Pedersen Fox (Architects of office tower) Yoshinori Nito + Dewhurst Macfarlane and Partners (Structural Engineers) Altieri Sebor Wieber (Mechanical Engineers) Kiltplan (Lighting Designers) 2x4 (Graphic Designers) Museum of Modern Art (Museum Programming and Technical Consultant to Mori Building)
ASSOC. ARCHITECT	Irie Miyake Architects & Engineers
ASSOC. STRUCTURAL ENGINEERS	Kozo Keikaku Engineers
CONTRACTOR	Kajima and Obayashi (Joints) Asahi Glass Company (Entry structure façade) Tripyramid (Entry structure stainless steel fittings)

JVC CULTURE, CONVENTION, AND BUSINESS CENTER
GUADALAJARA, MÉXICO

ARCHITECT	Carme Pinós Studio
CLIENT	Omnilife de Mexico S.A. de C.V.
DESIGN TEAM	Carme Pinós (Principal) Juan Antonio Andreu Samuel Arriola Rafael Balaguer Matteo Caravatti Philipp Hatzius Frédéric Jordan Cristina Ramos Pep Ripoll Pablo Saric Juan Miguel Tizon César Vergés Rodríguez
CONSULTANTS	Robert Brufau Associats, S.A. (Structural Engineer) Milian Associats S.A. (Contracting)

SOUTH-EAST COASTAL PARK AND AUDITORIUMS
BARCELONA, SPAIN

ARCHITECT	Foreign Office Architects
CLIENT	City of Barcelona
DESIGN TEAM	Farshid Moussavi (Principal) Alejandro Zaera-Polo (Principal) Nicolò Cadeo Peng Chua Ueli Degen Daniele Domeniconi Marco Guarnieri Jordi Pages Sergio Lopez- Piñeiro Terence Seah Daniel Valle Lluis Viu-Rebes
CONSULTANTS	Sergio Zampichelli (Associated Architect) Obiol, Moya y Asociados SL, Barcelona (Structural Engineer)

WESTERGASFABRIEK PARK
AMSTERDAM, THE NETHERLANDS

LANDSCAPE ARCHITECT	Gustafson Porter, Ltd
CLIENT	Projectbureau, Westergasfabriek, Westerpark District Council
DESIGN TEAM	Kathryn Gustafson (Principal) Neil Porter (Principal) Rene Vilijn Gerben Mienes Pauline Wieringa Mieke Tanghe Neil Black
CONSULTANTS	Steve Gaukroger, Northcroft, Belgium (Quantity Surveyor / Project Manager) Ian Carradice and Richard Bickers, Ove Arup and Partners (Civil Engineers)
ASSOC. ENGINEERS	Tauw Engineers Pietersbouwtechniek
CONTRACTOR	Marcus b.v.

Project Credits: Active Memory

MEMORIAL FOR THE MURDERED JEWS OF EUROPE
BERLIN, GERMANY

ARCHITECT	Eisenman Architects
CLIENT	Stiftung Denkmal fur die ermordeten Juden Europas
PROJECT MANAGER	Senatsverwaltung fur Stadtenwicklung Berlin
DESIGN TEAM	Peter Eisenman (Principal)
	Richard Rosson
	Lars Bachman
	Volker Bollig
	Constantin Doehler
	Nadine Homann
	Gordana Jakimovska
	Joerg Kiesow
	Jakob Ohm Laursen
	Yansong Ma
	Matias Musacchio
	Kai Petersen
	Wiebke Schneider
	Stephanie Streich
	Wolf von Trotha
	Federica Vannucchi
	Oliver Zorn
	Sebastian Mittendorfer
	Ingeborg Rocker
CONSULTANT	Buro Happold

WALTER SISULU SQUARE OF DEDICATION
KLIPTOWN, SOWETO, JOHANNESBURG, SOUTH AFRICA

ARCHITECT	StudioMAS Architecture and Urban Design
CLIENT	Johannesburg Development Agency & Blue IQ (Guateng Province)
DESIGN TEAM	Pierre Swanepoel (Principal)
	Precious Makwe
	Justin Snell
CONSULTANTS	Nomi Muthialu & Associates (Community) Nemai Consulting (Environmental)
	PD Naidoo (Traffic and Transportation)
	Herbert Prins (Heritage)
	Rob Taylor (Town Planner)
	Semenya Furumele (Infrastructure)
	Africa/ MJ Mboya/Boval Freeman Holley (Buildings)
	Arcus Gibb South Africa (Structural Engineers)
	Mahlati Ntene Lieberau (Surveyors)
	Palace Engineering (Electrical and Mechanical Engineers)
	Nat Mohlatlone (Surveyor)

MEMORIAL BRIDGE
RIJEKA, CROATIA

ARCHITECT	3LHD Architects
CLIENT	City of Rijeka, Croatia
DESIGN TEAM	Sasa Begovic (Principal)
	Marko Dabrovic (Principal)
	Tania Grozdanic (Principal)
	Silvije Novak (Principal)
	Sinisa Glusica
ASSOC. ARCHITECT	Osram Croatia
STRUCTURAL ENGINEER	CES (Bridge)
	Upi2m (Bench and handrail)
CONTRACTOR	GP KrK, Croatia (General)
	Shipyard 3rd May (Steel construction)
	Almes (Aluminum)

Project Credits: Temp Work

70 X 7 THE MEAL

Act XVI Bolzano, Italy, 2002
Act V-VII Mexico City, Mexico 2001
Act IV Diueze, France, 2001

ARTISTS	Lucy and Jorge Orta

BODY MOVIES

Schowburg Square, Rotterdam, the Netherlands, 2001
Hauptplatz, Linz, Austria, 2002
Williamson Square, Liverpool, United Kingdom, 2002

ARTIST	Rafael Lozano-Hemmer

PARIS PLAGE, PARIS. FRANCE, 2002-3

SCENOGRAPHER	Jean-Christophe Choblet

ANNUAL ARCHITECTURE COMMISSION
SERPENTINE GALLERY, LONDON, UNITED KINGDOM

ARCHITECTS	Oscar Niemeyer (2003)
	Toyo Ito with Arup (2002)
	Studio Libeskind with Arup (2001)
	Zaha Hadid Architects (2000)

THE GATES, CENTRAL PARK, NEW YORK, 2005

ARTISTS	Christo and Jeanne-Claude

Project Credits: Design Of/For/By the Public

NORTH MACADAM - MARQUAM HILL AERIAL TRAM INTERNATIONAL DESIGN COMPETITION, PORTLAND

SPONSOR
Portland Aerial Transportation, Inc. (PATI) / City of Portland

WINNING TEAM
Angelil/Graham/Pfenninger/Scholl Architecture (AGPS) with Ove Arup & Partners, Structural and Building Engineering, and Jane Wernick Associates, Structural Engineering.

JURY
J. Frano Violich, Charles Hoberman, Walter Hood, Diana Goldschmidt, Robert Frasca, Thomas Hacker.

SHAPING THE NEW AMERICAN RIVERFRONT INTERNATIONAL DESIGN COMPETITION, MEMPHIS

SPONSOR
Riverfront Development Corporation (RDC) / City of Memphis

WINNING TEAM
RTN Architects- Javier Rivarola, Gustavo Trosman, Ricardo Norton

JURY
Shauna Gillies Smith, John Gosling, Toni Griffin, William Morrish, Stanley Saitowitz, Dr. Willie W. Herenton (Mayor, City of Memphis), Kristi W. Jernigan, Dianne Dixon.

HARBOURFRONT PARKS AND OPEN SPACE DESIGN COMPETITION, TORONTO

SPONSOR
City of Toronto

WINNING TEAM
HTO- Janet Rosenberg Associates Landscape Architects Inc., Claude Cormier Architectes Paysagistes Inc., Harari Pontarini Architects, Sustainable Edge (Environmental Engineering), Beth Kapusta (Communications Consultant), William Greer (Heritage Advisor), Rina Greer (Public Art Consultant), Leni Schwendinger (Lighting Designer), and Janet Cardiff (Artist).

JURY
Vincent Asselin, Thomas Balsley, Larry Beasley, George Dark, Linda Irvine, Rocco Maragna, Susan Schelle.

BROOKLYN BRIDGE PARK

SPONSOR
Brooklyn Bridge Park Development Corporation (BBPDC)

WINNING TEAM
Michael Van Valkenburgh Associates Inc., lead; Accu-Cost Construction; Architecture Research Office; Battle McCarthy; Cerami Associates; Cooper, Robertson & Partnersn; DMJM + Harris, Marine; Domingo Gonzalez Associates, Inc.; Economics Research Associates; Eng-Wong Taub & Associates; Gensler; Ann Hamilton; Lynden B. Miller; Margie Ruddick Landscape; Maryann Thompson Architects; Matthews Neilsen Landscape Architects; Henry Bardsley, RFR; Robert France; Sol Lewitt; Ysreal A. Seinuck; James Carpenter Design Associates.

FRESH KILLS

SPONSOR
New York City Department of City Planning

WINNING TEAM
Field Operations, team leader; Skidmore, Owings & Merrill, project management; Hamilton, Rabinovitz & Alschuler (HR&A); AKRF, Inc.; Arup; Applied Ecological Services, Inc. (AES); GeoSyntec; Tomato; L'Observatoire International; Curry & Kerlinger; Richard Lynch; Mierle Laderman Ukeles.

FLUSHING-MEADOWS CORONA PARK

SPONSOR
NYC 2012

WINNING TEAM
Weiss/Manfredi Architects (Marion Weiss and Michael Manfredi, Partners; Christopher Payne; John Cooney; Kok Kian Goh; and Yehre Suh); Paul Manckewicz, Gaia Institute; Olin Partnership; Parsons Brinckerhoff Quade & Douglas, Inc.; Mara Ford

Photo Credits:

PLAZA UNBOUND (Page 26)

Aerial View of Oslo National Opera House, Oslo, Norway
RENDERING: SNØHETTA

View of Federation Square, Melbourne, Australia
PHOTO: ©LAB + BATES SMART

View of City Hall, London, United Kingdom
PHOTO: ©NIGEL YOUNG/ FOSTER AND PARTNERS

View of Ponte Parodi, Genoa, Italy
RENDERING: UN STUDIO

OPENING THE CITY (Page 40)

View of Poplar Street, Macon, Georgia
RENDERING: HOOD DESIGN

View of the Campinho favela, Rio de Janiero, Brazil
PHOTO: GABRIEL LEANDRO JÁUREGUI

View of raised public squares along the Alameda El Porvenir, Bogotá, Colombia
RENDERING: MGP ARQUITECTURA Y URBANISMO

INFORMATION IN PLACE (Page 54)

View of sketch of Fourth Grace, Liverpool, United Kingdom
DRAWING: ALSOP ARCHITECTS

Aerial view of one-north Singapore Science Hub
RENDERING: ZAHA HADID ARCHITECTS

View of the Institute of Contemporary Art, Fan Pier, Boston, Massachusetts
RENDERING: DILLER + SCOFIDIO

View of video screening auditorium at Intermedia Playground in Chungmuro Subway Station, Seoul, South Korea
PHOTO: JUNG-SIK MOON

NEW MEETING GROUNDS (Page 68)

View of detail of plan of Westergasfabriek Park, Amsterdam, the Netherlands
DRAWING: GUSTAFSON PORTER, LTD/ MECANOO ARCHITECTS

View of model of one of the bridge-buildings, JVC Culture, Convention and Business Center, Guadalajara, Mexico
PHOTO: EVA SERRAT

View of detail of the topography study for the South-East Coastal Park and Auditoriums, Barcelona, Spain
RENDERING: FOREIGN OFFICE ARCHITECTS

Aerial view of Island in the Mur, Graz, Austria
PHOTO: ELVIRA KLAMMINGER

View of the Museum Cone, Mori Art Museum, Roppongi Hills, Tokyo, Japan
PHOTO: GLUCKMAN MAYNER ARCHITECTS

ACTIVE MEMORY (Page 84)

View of the Memorial for the Murdered Jews of Europe, Berlin, Germany
PHOTO: EISENMAN ARCHITECTS

View of the Memorial Bridge, Rijeka, Croatia
PHOTO: 3LHD

View of Walter Sisulu Square of Dedication, Kliptown, Johannesburg, South Africa
RENDERING: FORESIGHT ANIMATION

OPEN: new designs for public space, Van Alen Institute, New York

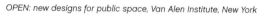

View of Southpoint, Roosevelt Island, showing the OPEN views:
Films on the City screening, August 2003

OPEN NEW DESIGNS FOR PUBLIC SPACE
VAN ALEN INSTITUTE

EXHIBITION DIRECTOR
Raymond W. Gastil

EXHIBITION CURATOR
Zoë Ryan

EXHIBITION DESIGN AND INSTALLATION
Freecell

EXHIBITION GRAPHIC DESIGN
Flat

THE PUBLIC SPACE ROUNDTABLES
Janet Abrams, Stan Allen, Paola Antonelli, Diana Balmori, Craig Barton,
Kadambari Baxi, Andrew Darrell, Lisa Frigand, Tony Hiss,
Andrea Kahn, Jerold Kayden, Bart Lootsma, Anuradha Mathur,
Elizabeth Mossop, Max Page, Anne Pasternak, Sherida Paulsen,
Mark Robbins, Ben Rubin, James S. Russell, James Sanders,
Craig Schwitter, Nasrine Seraji, Peter Slatin, David Small, Michael
Sorkin, Marian Starr Imperatore, Lisa Strausfeld, Gwendolyn Wright

VAI EXHIBITION TEAM
Jonathan Cohen-Litant
Alan Brake
Arif Durakovic
Marcus Woollen

INSTALLATION TEAM
Corey Yurkovich
Mina Talai
Darren Guyer
Josh Young
Glen Barfield

RESEARCH ASSISTANTS
Hillary Angelo
Sonya Lee

SPONSORS
The Andy Warhol Foundation for the Visual Arts

*This project is funded in part by a grant from the
National Endowment for the Arts*

*This exhibition is made possible with public funds from the
New York State Council on the Arts, a state agency*

The Stephen A. and Diana L. Goldberg Foundation

Special thanks to

VAN ALEN INSTITUTE

Van Alen Institute is committed to improving the design of the public realm. Since it began its program of Projects in Public Architecture in fall 1995, the Institute has directed exhibitions, design studies and competitions, lectures, conferences, and publications designed to research and communicate the critical role of design in regenerating cities. While the Institute's projects are grounded in the challenges and opportunities in New York, the projects are structured to engage an interdisciplinary and state, nation, and worldwide array of practitioners, policy-makers, students, educators, and civic leaders. Each project, from an ideas competition for Governors Island in 1996 to OPEN: new designs for public space, is designed to be a catalyst for changing perceptions and possibilities for the future of public life.

The Institute is able to undertake this program thanks to its board of trustees, membership, and the generous support of public, private, and civic organizations, as well as the support of its specific project partners, including community boards, city and state agencies, universities, publishers, and museums and design centers.
The Institute, a non-profit charitable organization, welcomes tax-deductible support, whether general or project-based. The Institute is named for William Van Alen, the architect of the Chrysler Building, and the Institute's most significant historic benefactor.